SURVIVING ADVERSITY

Cover and Book Design by : Scott Helmer
Website Design by: Tony Stocco

www.survivingadversity.com

Printed and bound in Canada, first printing March 2004

National Library of Canada Cataloguing in Publication

Carley, Gord, 1962-
        Surviving adversity : 32 stories that reveal the power of hope / Gord Carley.

ISBN 0-9734162-0-3 (pbk.)

    1. Life change events. 2. Hope. I. Title.

BF637.L53C37 2003   158.1
C2003-905998-7

ACKNOWLEDGEMENTS

I would like to thank the thirty-two individuals who have shared their stories in the hope that by publicizing their experiences they might help others.

I would also like to express my appreciation to everyone who has taken the time to read earlier drafts of this book and provide me with feedback. I owe a special thank you to my family and friends, who over the years have been so supportive.

Without the advice and understanding of my wife Andra, this book would not have been completed. I dedicate this book to her and to our daughter, Meg.

CONTENTS

CONTENTS

CONTENTS

CONTENTS

INTRODUCTION

Within five years of completing university, I had started and sold a publication for just under one million dollars. I thought I was set for life.

I was born on December 10, 1962, the youngest in a family of four. Most of my childhood was spent participating in sports or playing games with my parents and siblings. Worries were virtually non-existent.

My father and I had a close relationship, partly because my father, after enduring a third heart attack, began working fewer hours and spending much of his spare time driving me around the province to play baseball. Often we would travel a couple of hours to games that were in obscure small towns with rundown facilities. We drove on country roads that all seemed the same and listened to radio broadcasts of Montreal Expo baseball games. With each twist in the road the reception would drift in and out on the crackling AM station. The tie between my love of baseball and the memory of my father remains unbreakable to this day.

He died of heart failure July 1st, 1983. The most difficult moment that weekend was after the service, watching people walk away from the grave and realizing that for most of them, life was continuing on that day, while I would have to live the rest of my life without my dad. I was twenty years old and looking back now, I can see that his death had a greater impact on me than I thought at the time.

I returned to university and graduated in 1984 with a business degree. I despised the concept of being just a number in a corporation and promised myself that I would never work in one. I was hired as a salesman by a very small company that imported electronic signs displaying moving advertisements. In my first ten weeks I only sold three signs, which resulted in me earning less than $100 per week. At this pace, my entire savings would be depleted in a few months.

Luckily there was one big sale pending—a twenty sign package—that would generate $6,000 in commissions. It appeared to be a done deal provided the product worked during a presentation to the Vice President of a bank. I brought a programmer with me to the meeting in case the sign malfunctioned. When he turned the machine on, I watched in horror. Instead of seeing relevant banking information such as interest rates scroll across the screen, I watched as stick figures made love in different positions on the moving message board. Without telling me, the programmer had decided this would be funny and might help to break the ice. There was no laughter, and we were asked to leave the office immediately. The sale fell through and I resigned from the company two weeks later.

I needed the financial security that a salary offered, so I took a job selling labels for a printing company. After three years, I began to investigate an idea for a free newspaper that contained only classified ads relating to employment. Exhaustive research proved to me that it might succeed, so I decided to take a chance and start it. It was financed with a combination of my savings, a friend's investment, a bank loan, and a family loan. During the day, I sold ads with my staff of six and at night I would place newspaper boxes on city streets. It was a grueling pace. The fear of failure was a greater driving force than my desire for success. I fantasized that the business would allow me to earn $100,000 per year.

The first issue was published September 4, 1988, and the new venture made money from the second week on. After six months, a friend advised me that the value of my business was likely four times the profit that could be earned for the year. Selling the paper for cash and avoiding the uncertainty and risks of the future seemed logical to me because my outlook tended to be "live for today." In my wildest dreams, I never envisioned that I might achieve financial success so quickly.

I sold 75% of the business in May of 1989, just eleven months after it had been started, for $660,000. A capital gains exemption meant that $500,000 of the proceeds was tax-free. I later sold the final 25% of the business for an additional $200,000. I was set for life!

One month after selling the business, I rented a luxurious penthouse apartment on the 37th floor of a waterfront condominium where each room offered a beautiful view of the glistening waters of Lake Ontario. It was furnished well beyond anything I could have imagined. My cramped, cockroach infested apartment with its purple bedsofa was a thing of the past. The extreme pressure, responsibilities, and worries that came with starting a business were replaced by a constant feeling of satisfaction and seemingly permanent elation.

I never saw the impending crash until it was too late.

In January 1990, a business acquaintance introduced the idea of publishing a directory containing advertisements of products targeted to homeowners. I jumped at it. Without discussing my plans with anyone, or researching the market, the cost to produce it or any other aspect of the business, I hired four sales reps, set up an office and proceeded. Costs were higher than expected and by the end of 1991, I had lost over $400,000. Each month seemed worse than the previous one. My ego was bruised, but I was tenacious and did not want to give up or admit to the world that I was fallible.

I married my girlfriend whom I had dated on and off for eight years in March of 1992, rather than risk losing her because she was running out of patience with me. I also formed a partnership with an entrepreneur who had both money to invest and a complementary idea that might turn the struggling consumer directories around. A few months later, the business partner confided that he could not meet the agreed investment terms. This disaster put me deeply into debt. That same year, I found out an employee had taken the liberty to write cheques to himself. For the first time in my life, creditors were calling for money that I could not find. I felt like a phony because all my friends believed I was doing better than I actually was. I did not let on otherwise.

I had gone from euphoria to deep depression. My net worth of nearly one million dollars had disappeared. I now owed over $220,000 to a multitude of creditors and my marriage was also failing. I could not comprehend how things could change so quickly.

In July 1993, I separated from my wife and moved into a new apartment that had only two lamps, a footstool, a mattress, and a few pieces of cutlery. Despite my battered self-esteem and tremendous guilt over the dissolution of the marriage, I had an overwhelming sense of certainty that I had finally made a good decision. It felt as if the sun was partially shining again. I was happy once more!

I wanted to avoid bankruptcy if at all possible. I sold my two remaining publications to pay a small portion of the debts, and started working as a salaried publisher for a large corporation, a place I had promised myself I would always avoid. However, the security of a steady cheque far outweighed the self-created stigma of being a number.

Simple business tasks like taking a client to lunch became stressful ordeals because I would have to scramble to find a way to pay for it. I never had a corporate credit card because my employer used the same credit card company that was threatening to take me to collections. To pay for the lunch, I would free up $30 on a personal credit card that was at its limit by paying it off through another line of credit that was also "maxed" out, knowing that the transaction would not hit for a day. I would then tell the client I had already eaten so as to be sure the bill would not exceed $30.

My best memory during this time was finding a jar of coins that contained about $40. This was a huge windfall, and worth the risk to my pride at being seen cashing them at a bank near work.

One of the most difficult things for me was adjusting to the reality that I was totally broke, driving a car that was about to fall apart, and unable to afford to go out to events with my friends. I kept my plight secret from family, friends, and even a steady girlfriend who was my closest confidant mainly because I was so embarrassed to have been given so much and then to have lost it.

I spent more of my free time watching television and one week I ended up viewing five biographies of entrepreneurs. Each person had failed multiple times. They had been in far worse situations than I had, both financially and personally, yet somehow they had all recovered from massive indebtedness. Many well-known, successful businessmen had all been there before me. Perspective finally hit home and I accepted emotionally what I knew intuitively, which was that I was not alone. It was the moment when I first began to hope that my circumstances might change for the better.

Gaining the perspective that I was not unique in succeeding and then failing in spectacular fashion allowed me to begin to hope. I dreamed of the day I would be out of debt and thought of it every moment. Beginning to hope created a mindset and certainty that I would succeed.

A long five-year battle began: I would chip away at my debts, and seem to make headway only to get hit with an unexpected bill or an interest and penalty charge from the past that I had ignored. This was best typified when I paid off one of my Visa cards only to learn that I owed over $6000 to the government.

Many days were awful. Several times one major creditor had their lawyer meet with me and threaten to put me into bankruptcy unless I paid the remaining balance at a faster pace. Each time, I would have to go through a degrading process to prove that I had no money to give them, but was trying to pay, anyway.

I finally achieved in 1998 what I had fantasized about every day for five years: I paid off the last of my debts. I had thought of this moment thousands of times, and had planned many different ways to celebrate it, yet when I delivered the last payment to my only remaining creditor I simply felt contentment. There was an overwhelming sense of pride within me because I had persevered.

There were several practical ideas and actions that helped me in my darkest days when I was drowning in debt. I always found something to look forward to each day. As silly as it may sound, breakfast was that something for me. I ate my bowl of cereal and toast in peace, oblivious to how bad the upcoming day would be, or how many creditors might call me. I completely enjoyed that time. Often the day would go downhill immediately after that meal, but I knew that there would be another breakfast the next day. There is always something, even if it's small, that you can look forward to.

Taking responsibility for everything was critical. Friends who have heard my story have asked, "Why should you be blamed for an employee spending money that had not been authorized?" My answer has always been that, had proper financial checks and balances been in place, none of it would have happened. Accepting that I was partially responsible for creating many of my challenges made me feel that I had some control, and did not allow me to blame others for my difficulties.

Recalling past successes and reminding myself of my best qualities helped me to stay positive despite the bumps that came along the way. I kept visualizing myself as recovering and making some progress each day even though it often seemed that each step forward was accompanied by one or two steps back. Being able to laugh at myself throughout the bad years also made it easier on my sanity and kept my attitude upbeat.

Initially, it was tough admitting that I could mess up my life so badly. I was very embarrassed and ashamed to have hurt people's feelings by failing at marriage, and in business to have squandered so much money. It is not always easy, but you need to forgive yourself for past mistakes. Now I put less pressure on myself and accept that if the perfect role model were centered on the equator, then I would be found on the fringes of the Arctic, continually trying to move south towards the equator. I know I'm aimed in the right direction, but sometimes I feel like I am traveling at the speed of a glacier. All I can do is keep trying to improve and remind myself that no one is perfect.

One major and potentially devastating error I made was not to tell anyone about my troubles. If I had to do it over again, I would tell a few family members and friends. It would have been much easier to share my situation instead of keeping it secret. My challenge was so small compared to what others have faced, and yet, at the time it was all encompassing for me. Holding all my troubles inside distorted my outlook and made everything seem far worse than it was.

Gaining perspective allowed me to hope, and once this happened, I created positive momentum and my financial recovery took hold. The moment a situation appears futile is precisely when perspective and the presence of hope will make the biggest difference.

****

After paying the last of my creditors, I started to think about writing a book that would analyze how other people had overcome adversity. In 1998, I met with seven individuals who had experienced diverse challenges. The book was put on hold when I moved to Minnesota to start a business and it was not until two and a half years later that I was able to resume working on it. I developed a list of prospective interview candidates by first noting all the different types of adversity that one might encounter. I then searched for people that fit within each category of adversity. Many charitable organizations also helped by providing me with leads. Finally, I contacted the various names that I had researched and set up interviews. I was very surprised to discover what the common thread was in their stories.

I hope that you will find the following profiles uplifting and that the advice offered in the thirty-two chapters is beneficial and helps you to conquer life's challenges.

CHAPTER ONE

GERALD COFFEE

I ejected at 680 miles per hour and was knocked unconscious by the impact of the jet stream.

****

Gerald Coffee and his crewman, Robert Hanson, were shot down on February 3, 1966 while flying a mission over North Vietnam.

****

I was born June 2, 1934 and grew up in Modesto, California. My father worked for large construction companies, and my mother was a homemaker who later became a secretary for the school district. My father had polio, which left him with a withered right arm and a shorter leg, but it never slowed him down. It was not an issue in the family nor did he get any special consideration. I realize now that my dad was an inspiration to me. He was my hero.

In high school, I was athletic and active in the student government. My self-confidence was strong, thanks to my parents, and I had been taught good values. They took me to swim meets, football games and skiing trips to the Sierras. I would have to describe my upbringing as "All-American."

I majored in art at UCLA and after graduating in 1957, I signed up with the Navy, which allowed me to procrastinate from entering the real world. I liked the Navy and after two years I received my wings and was sent to a light reconnaissance group where I flew a Crusader, which was a variation of the fighter plane. I served three years in that squadron flying from the US Saratoga in the Mediterranean, the Caribbean, and the North Atlantic.

During the Cuban missile crisis I was on the first mission that flew over Cuba. I took the photos that Adlai Stevenson later used in the United Nations to prove that Russia had installed missile sites. We actually saw the missile launchers and the missiles stacked like wood alongside one another. There was no problem spotting or identifying them. Flying at 400-500 feet, we knew we had found the right place because we could see the launch pad and tracks where a missile could be positioned, the trucks designed to transport them, as well as miscellaneous electronic equipment and radar. The Soviets had tried to pull a fast one!

I went over to Vietnam in December 1965 and flew missions from the US Kitty Hawk in the Tonkin Gulf. While flying on February 3, 1966, a sensation occurred similar to driving a car across a speedbump at 60 miles per hour. Since the air was smooth, I immediately assumed we had taken a hit. The warning lights came on and then the hydraulic pressure gauges flickered. I started to lose power. The controls got very sluggish. My plane had been hit by anti-aircraft fire over North Vietnam and the hydraulic system was disabled.

We were at 4,000 feet when we took the hit. The plane rolled uncontrollably and started to go down. I told my crewman Robert Hanson to eject. By that time, the plane's speed had picked up to 680 miles per hour. When I ejected, I was knocked unconscious.

I regained consciousness in the water, where somehow I had inflated my survival flotation devices while drifting in and out of consciousness. Almost immediately, Vietnamese boats were coming to pick me up. They were firing at me mostly to intimidate me from trying to escape. I think they knew they couldn't hit me from that far away, and when they got closer they stopped firing. After being pulled out of the water, we were strafed by U.S. attack planes from the Kitty Hawk who didn't realize I was in the Vietnamese boat.

My first feeling upon being captured was one of classic denial. I was very groggy and probably suffering from a concussion. My elbow was shattered, my right forearm was fractured, my shoulder was dislocated, and I also had many cuts and burns. I worried about whether Robert Hanson had managed to eject safely.

Over the next twelve days, under the cover of darkness, I was taken north to Hanoi and into Hoa Lo Prison. The first year was the toughest as I realized what was going on in my life, and asked, "Why me, God?" It was very tough dealing with emotional factors.

I was tortured three to four times per year, until 1970 when the North changed their policy on this. They would interrogate me, and I would refuse to talk so then they would bind my upper arms tightly with parachute shrouds which were tighter than ropes and pull my hands behind me, put a bar over my ankles and feet, and then pull, cutting off all circulation, to the point where it felt like my upper body would split open. The captor would then put a foot on the back of my neck so that my ears were between my big toes.

My shoulders were being separated and there was tremendous pain from lack of circulation. Then they put a hook in the ceiling and hoisted me up, so that all my weight was on my arms. I was twisted in all directions; it was as if they were playing tetherball with me.

Other times, they would put me on a high stool and let me sit there for days without sleep and with ankles cuffed to the rungs of the stool. When I would fall over, they would shove me back up on it.

I was most vulnerable at the beginning when I was injured and in solitary confinement. Even though I knew intuitively that there were others, it was a huge relief when I made my first contact with another prisoner. We communicated by knocking on the walls using a tap code that was highly developed. This allowed us to converse, share information, jokes, and stories, as well as talking about families and the future. The tap code was based on a 25-letter matrix. The guards knew in theory how it worked, but when some of the English interpreters tried to listen, we went so fast and used so much slang that they could never keep up.

I was optimistic 80% of the time, and the other 20% I was pretty low. There were peaks and valleys. Not knowing how long I would be there allowed me to hope that I would be home for each holiday and birthday.

Spiritual faith was essential. In solitary, even in my darkest moments, I felt that I was not alone and this allowed me to find a little strength. At one prison I stayed in, someone had written on the wall, God=Strength, which summarized it well.

After eighteen months I received my first letter from my wife. It told me that my youngest son, Jerry Jr. had been born two months after I was shot down. He joined three other children we had before I left for Vietnam. Receiving the letter brought a mixture of emotions, but mainly indescribable joy.

From 1968 on, the bombing of North Vietnam was more intense. I felt that the pressure of more bombing, would be the only thing they would respond to. In 1972, Hanoi was bombed from December 10 through December 29, which led to the peace pact in Paris. Finally after seven years in prison, it appeared that I was going to be freed. All the POWs were assembled in the prison courtyard where the prison commander told us we would be released in two-week increments. The sick would be first to go and then it would be in order of when we were shot down. We would not accept any other way.

I was bussed to the airport with fellow POWs, where there was a small ceremony under a parachute canopy. We then boarded a transport plane and were served by four beautiful nurses who gave us coffee, donuts and newspapers. We were still walking on eggs because we were afraid that something might happen to screw up the process. It was almost too much to hope that it would be true.

As the engines started up, we all became quiet, thinking, "Is it really going to happen?" The plane taxied to the runway and then revved the engines. It vibrated as the brakes were released and it began to move down the runway. I was straining against the shoulder harness thinking, "Come on you beast, get airborne, get airborne." Finally the nose came up and we felt the wheels leave the runway. The pilot came over the intercom and said, "Congratulations gentlemen, we've just left North Vietnam!" And only then did we cheer. We were in shock and hugging each other.

It was a joy to finally have hot showers and good food. I flew from the base in the Philippines to Florida to meet my family. My wife had kept my image alive and the kids were great. I finally met my son Jerry Jr. who was by then seven years old.

In my absence we had landed a man on the moon, area codes were now needed to dial direct, and even my most respected friends had long hair and beards. I woke up in a different society and wondered, "How the hell did I get here?"

I had to build a tough shell around me while in Vietnam, convincing myself on a daily basis that I was right to be there and that our cause was just. Upon returning, I realized that I was in the minority who held this view. There was no respect for authority and a lack of love for our country, all of which, I found very difficult to accept. I was struck by the negative feelings about the Vietnam War. As well, rebuilding my relationship with my wife proved difficult and we divorced twelve years later.

In 1988, I watched my former crewman Robert Hanson's casket being lowered from the plane after it had been released by the Communist government in Hanoi. It was surreal because in my mind I had put this all to rest. It was also a bittersweet experience, for on the one hand, his fate was resolved. I knew his family would feel that way. On the other hand, it was very sad because he was in his early twenties when he was killed and now would have been in his early forties. I thought about the life that might have been. He had earned glory by sacrificing his life for the cause of freedom and helping a rather unsophisticated country try to protect itself and build its own democracy. A myriad of things went through my mind that day.

As I look back, I am not angry with the majority of my captors who were only doing their jobs. No matter what the color of skin, the shape of eyes, the sound of language spoken, we all laugh, cry, hunger, thirst, and want the same things for family and loved ones. You cannot let the objects of bitterness keep control of you.

You must find purpose in adversity and recognize that you have skills, wisdom, and the fortitude to do whatever you need to do in order to survive. Having faith that you will find a purpose in what is happening to you, and then capitalizing on it is going beyond survival. There is a hero in all of us. There is nothing extraordinary about me. If I can do it so can you.

****

Captain Gerald Coffee retired in 1985, and now is a motivational speaker who shares his story with audiences worldwide.

CHAPTER TWO

JACKIE PFLUG

Thirty minutes into the flight, three men stood up with guns and grenades.

****

Jackie Pflug was a passenger on EgyptAir Flight 648, which left Athens on Thanksgiving weekend 1985.

****

In 1985, my husband Scott and I were teaching at the Cairo American school. On Thanksgiving weekend, Scott and his students went to Athens to attend a volleyball tournament for four days. I joined Scott for the weekend and left Athens the day before he and his students were scheduled to leave.

EgyptAir Flight 648 departed at nine in the morning. Thirty minutes into the flight, three men stood up with guns and grenades. We were 35,000 feet in the air. The flight attendant came on the intercom and announced that we had been hijacked by the "Egypt Revolution", and if we did what we were told, then no one would be hurt. I believed that.

The hijackers were screaming in broken English, telling us to sit down and shut up. It was very chaotic. They started to collect passports from the passengers. Halfway back there were three undercover sky marshals. One of the marshals reached for his gun when asked for his passport and bullets started to fly, puncturing the aircraft. The cabin depressurized and the oxygen masks descended as the pilot brought the plane to a lower altitude. He was forced to make an emergency landing in Malta.

That is when the negotiations started. The Maltese officials demanded that all the passengers be released. The hijackers wanted to go to Beirut and they warned that they would execute a passenger every fifteen minutes starting first with Israelis and next with Americans.

About twenty minutes after we landed, the lead hijacker grabbed a woman and put a gun to her head. The passengers in the front could see what was happening. I was sitting in the back when I heard a gunshot. The man beside me said, "Oh my goodness, he shot her and threw her down the staircase." Fifteen minutes later they shot another Israeli woman and it became very clear what was happening. I could not believe they were doing this. I knew Egyptians respected women and held them in high regard, so I had thought we would be OK. This hope left me because the first few people executed were women.

The hijackers tied my hands behind my back. I was taken with two other passengers, Scarlet and Patrick, who were also Americans, and seated in the first row. I sat by the window. I kept thinking about whether I had told people close to me that I loved them enough, and concluded that I had not. Patrick was shot first, then Scarlet.

I had grown up a Catholic and had gone to church every Sunday and was still a strong spiritual person. I had always felt that God protected me. I knew that didn't mean I would not get hurt in any way; it just meant that I was being watched over. I closed my eyes and prayed to God for my life. A peaceful, tranquil feeling came over me and I felt I would be fine. If I lived it would be OK and if I died I would be OK, too. I also felt that God was saying, "You do not understand this, but someday you might find a reason for it."

They brought me to the front of the plane and opened the door. I looked at my world for what I believed would be the last time. It was a beautiful day with blue sky and puffy clouds, and I thought what a terrible thing this was to be happening on such a day.

My intellect was telling me to try to knock them down, and then throw my body down the staircase. But then some voice inside me said, "Do not worry, it will be OK. Everything in life will be OK no matter what the outcome." It was almost as if I gave up and put everything in God's hands. I was in shock. That is when he put the gun to my head and shot me.

I did not feel anything as I fell twenty-five feet from the metal stairs of the plane onto the ground. I was sprawled facedown on the airport tarmac with a bullet in my head and my blood slowly draining onto the cement.

I was semiconscious when the vision of my grandmother came to me in spirit as a bright whiteness. She said, "It's time to go." I lifted out of my body and went with her. She was leading me through a dark tunnel towards light. I had an awareness that I was leaving earth and I could see myself lying on the tarmac below. Something was telling me that it was not time for me to go yet so I told her that I loved her and then she let me go. She went into the white light while I came back into my body. After five hours I was picked up by an airport grounds crew, who at first assumed I was dead.

I spent time in hospitals in Malta and Germany before being transferred back in early December to the United States. Recovering from the injuries caused by the bullet was a long-term process both physically and mentally. In the years after the hijacking, I had to battle a brain injury that left me with no short-term memory, near-blindness, and epilepsy that caused seizures. The other big challenge for me was overcoming the event itself.

My marriage ended three years after the hijacking. We had only been married for five months when it happened. Our union was not strong enough to survive the event and the subsequent recovery.

Tragedy catapults you into another way of thinking. Before the hijacking I did not keep commitments and only did things that I wanted to do. I was thirty years old when it happened and thought that life was about friends, laughs, and having the right car and clothes. I was off visiting one country after another by myself. Now I want to be with people and loved ones. My adventurous spirit has never died but I do not need it to make me happy. If you ask my parents or friends, they would say they see me as the "old Jackie," but I think my integrity has changed a lot for the better.

Now I ask myself before I go to sleep: "Did I live with integrity today, did I laugh and smile a lot, talk to someone I did not know, and did I move closer to my goals?" Each night I write down five things that I am grateful for. I constantly tell people how much I love them, and I try to resolve disputes before traveling. Now, when I fly, I can honestly say I have no regrets. I look back at the hijacking as a wakeup call to pay more attention to what life is all about.

Today, when I think back to my out of body experience in Malta, I remember the beauty and peacefulness of it and I am comforted that loved ones ahead of us are all OK.

People's perceptions of difficult times vary. They could range from cancer or debts to divorce. An obstacle that leaves you devastated may be something I just brush off. Whatever the situation, never give up and get the help you need along the way.

Look around to see who you perceive as strong and follow them. Do what they do. If you want to be fit, go to the person who is fit and ask them what they do every day and then follow their advice. If you want to be at peace with yourself, then follow a person with strong faith, and rely on your faith.

****

Jackie Pflug was the fifth passenger on EgyptAir Flight 648 to be shot in the head and thrown down the stairs onto the tarmac. The hijacking continued until the plane was stormed by Egyptian Commandos. Fifty-nine passengers died during the ordeal.

Eleven years after the hijacking, Jackie was finally able to forgive the hijackers and by doing so, release the hold they had on her. She has since remarried and has one son. Today, she has rehabilitated herself to a point where she travels the country speaking to groups and advising teachers and students on educational issues.

CHAPTER THREE

DREW PEARSON

In just over one month, my charmed life had been turned upside down.

****

Drew Pearson played professional football for the Dallas Cowboys. During his eleven-year career, he played in three Super Bowls and was an All-Pro three times. He was named by the Pro Football Hall of Fame to its NFL All-Decade team of the 70's.

****

I was born Jan 12, 1951, and grew up in South River, New Jersey. I was the third of seven kids, with three brothers and three sisters. My father pushed all of the boys into sports and made it easy for us to participate, by saying that if we did not go to practice after school, then we would have to go to work.

Growing up, I was only interested in baseball, basketball, and football. I read every sports section and followed all the players, even ones on local high school teams. I found ways to play baseball by myself by going to the schoolyard with a sponge ball and throwing it against the wall at a strike zone that I had drawn. In my mind, I would strike out the entire New York Yankee team, beating a lineup that had Mickey Mantle and Roger Maris.

Our family had a strong faith, and my mother was the leader in this regard. I would sneak out of church to play ball, so finally she worked out an agreement where I could play on Sundays if I went to church on Wednesdays.

I was recruited by several universities to play football, and I shocked a lot of people by choosing to attend the University of Tulsa, which was a smaller school. After my freshman season ended, the coach told me I could start as a quarter-back but I chose to play receiver instead because at the time, there were not many black athletes who were getting the chance to play quarterback in professional football.

After graduating in 1973, I made the Dallas Cowboys as an undrafted free agent. The pinnacle of my professional career was playing in the Super Bowl. I was proud of our team because we worked hard and overcame so many barriers throughout the season. Stepping out of the tunnel to run onto the field at the Super Bowl, and hearing the crowd cheer for me, gave me a feeling of invincibility.

Being on the winning side of a Super Bowl, and having performed at that high level, was a tremendously satisfying feeling because I had accomplished the ultimate goal I had set for myself. To be able to say, "I have reached the top, there is no more I can do and there is no next game to play" is fantastic.

Towards the end of my career, my teammate and friend Billy Joe Dupree said, "Everything that Drew touches turns to gold," which seemed to be true, as everything was falling into place. At the time, I was playing in Super Bowls, getting individual recognition, and living a charmed life. This was about to change quickly.

In February of 1984, my wife and I divorced. I gave her almost everything because I did not want our two kids, who were nine and five, to suffer financially. I could afford to do that because I knew I had tremendous earning power. At the time, I was negotiating a new contract with the Dallas Cowboys that would put me in the upper echelon in the league as far as salaries went.

One month later, on March 22, 1984, I was involved in a car accident and lost my youngest brother, Carey, who was riding with me. I was ripped up internally really badly, hemorrhaging, and in critical condition for three or four days.

Trying to deal with the loss of my brother, and with the guilt of why it was him and not me, was very tough. I really did not care that because of the injuries, I had to give up my football career. If that was what I had to sacrifice, so what? It seemed like a very trivial thing to lose. My brother had to give up his life.

It was the lowest point in my life. My family was my support group. They came down to Dallas after they buried my brother in New Jersey and were there the whole time for me. My mother and I had some great talks where she put the tragedy into a religious perspective. This comforted me because the guilt was so heavy. I felt like I was responsible for taking Carey away from my family. Without a doubt, my faith helped me through this time by providing constant encouragement, as I prayed and asked for forgiveness.

After I retired from football, I was picked up by CBS Sports as an announcer, and voted rookie of the year by USA Today. However, after the first year, CBS decided not to renew my contract. Terry Bradshaw was coming along at the same time, and they decided to cultivate him instead of me. This bothered me tremendously because if I was good enough to be the best rookie announcer, I thought I should have a chance to get better in the second year. I started to wonder what I was going to do.

I worked hard to get back into shape, thinking I might have a chance to make a comeback with Dallas. In the team physical, both the doctor and a national liver specialist approved me to play. The specialist said the odds were 99% that if I got hit and hemorrhaged, I would be OK, but in my mind, to be the player I had been, I needed a 100% endorsement.

Coach Landry asked me to assist the receivers in training camp and to stay on as a coach during the season. Football coaches are unappreciated and work very hard. I helped out, but realized I did not love football enough to continue coaching.

I decided to contact two guys who had been asking me to join them in starting a sport apparel business. That is when Drew Pearson Enterprises, which later became Drew Pearson Marketing, Inc. was born. We decided to sell only headware because everyone was selling T-shirts, and we did not have the resources to handle a wide variety of products.

Our office was in one of the partner's homes when we started. There were serious times when we were not making money, had no salary or cash flow, and could not pay our three-person staff. My partners, Ken Shead and Mike Russell, kept saying, "We will make this work; our time will come."

We were close to folding the business when we received the good news that the 1988 U.S. Olympic committee had chosen us to be their supplier. We were shocked and looked at each other and said, "Now what do we do?" It gave us instant credibility and opened up doors for a deal with Disney, which came next. In July 1989, after six months of negotiating, we signed an agreement with an apparel company that infused significant capital into our business, which helped us turn the corner.

Adversity is part of life. We could be white, black, red, green, big or small, right or left handed, but one thing we have in common is that in our lives we will have to face adversity in some form or shape.

I look at adversity as an obstacle, and try to see what I can do to make myself better or stronger, so I can overcome it. When you are facing difficult times and it does not look like you will make it, that is when you need to keep pulling and plugging, because you never know when that one additional phone call or extra effort will get you over the hump. I am a perfect example of that, because in business, we could have folded the tent a long time ago and we would never have known how close we were to making it happen. A lot of people give up when a little extra effort or push is all that is needed.

Faith is, without a doubt, a critical factor. You have to believe in something that is greater than yourself. It certainly played a key part in helping me overcome everything I have faced.

I think of adversity through a football analogy: If I catch a pass, and the defense tries to tackle me, I never go down on the first hit, because I always try to give that extra effort and get the additional yard. It applies to life, too. You are going to get hit, but you do not need to go down. Keep trying, and you will get the extra yard or maybe score the touchdown.

****

Today, Drew Pearson Marketing, Inc. is a flourishing organization. It has had yearly revenues reaching $77 million and been rated as high as the fifteenth largest Black-owned business by Black Enterprise Magazine.

CHAPTER FOUR

BRENDA O'QUIN

I ran to the door and found a police officer standing on my front porch.

****

Brenda O'Quin was happily married and the mother of two boys aged twenty-two and seventeen.

****

My confidence was pretty typical for a girl growing up, in that it was up and down, depending upon such "major things" as how the dress looked on me that day. I had lots of friends, and in the late 60s and early 70s we partied and lived it up. I had a really good time in college where I did a four-year journalism degree at the University of North Texas.

I met my future husband Alex in college. He did a tour of duty in Vietnam as a gunner on a helicopter, and in 1970, while he was back for R and R, we got married in Hawaii. He went back to Vietnam after our wedding and when he returned he was a very different person because he had started to abuse substances and alcohol. We had two children, Jason who was born in 1973 and Michael in 1978, before splitting up in 1979. It was a ten-year relationship that should have lasted a year.

After the divorce, his parents and my family helped me as I tried to work each day and raise the children. It was very difficult financially but Jason, Michael, and I were very close. They were quite involved in sports and overall it was a very happy time and they seemed to do OK. Even when they were little and I was working, I would always be at the school for activities. Occasionally I was the only parent who showed up. I remarried in 1985. My new husband Bill had two children who were older than my boys, and also a seventy-year-old mother who lived with him.

On Friday August 26, 1995, Jason and I went out to eat. Michael met us at the restaurant to pick up his allowance. Michael, who was now seventeen years old, and his friend Katy, went out to a party. After they left the party, Michael and Katy dropped a friend off and then instead of going two hundred yards down the road to Katy's house, they decided to get some food at Whataburger.

After eating, Michael was asked by two people he knew casually if he would give them a ride home. Once in the car, they pulled a gun and drove Michael and Katy to a desolate area twenty or thirty minutes away. The younger one, a fifteen-year-old, held the gun on Michael. Michael said to them, "Just take the car stereo" which was all they wanted. The fifteen-year-old told him that he felt Michael would tell, so they shot him in the chest and head, which Katy had to watch. The gun jammed when they turned it on her, but then the other boy, an eighteen-year-old, got the gun and shot her. They left Michael's car by the side of the road and took the stereo system.

The stereo system was sold the next day for $260.

The sun was coming up when the doorbell rang. A police officer was at the door and he told me that Michael had been killed. My first reaction was shock. I could not believe it because I thought I had heard Michael come in the night before. I was in a fog and it took a while to sink in.

The Monday after the murder we were in court, which was the morning of Katy's funeral, and the day before Michael's funeral. We had to be at a hearing to ensure the fifteen-year-old would not be released on bail and given to his family. In my mind it would have been dangerous for him because many people close to me were enraged.

The adult court system takes forever. The first trial was a year after the murder and the second trial was a year and a half later. We were forced to relive the tragedy all over again when the trials occurred. Both boys were charged with capital murder and sentenced to a minimum of forty years before parole. I was OK with them having to spend the rest of their lives in prison. I was indifferent to capital punishment. Also, I did not want to keep getting pulled into court, which is what happens when the death penalty is given.

It was really sad. One of the mothers would come by herself and sit in support of her son but she testified in an honest manner, which was not helpful to her son. After it was over, she asked one of my son's friends to pass along an apology and we ended up talking to her later. The other family was just the opposite. It was as if they felt that we had done something wrong and were saying, "How dare we bring their son into court."

I had worked with kids on probation before, and had lined up a therapist to help families whose kids had been murdered. Ironically, our family and Katy's were the first to use the therapist. One of the emotions you go through is not anger but rage. You have to find a way to let go, otherwise the murderers who control your life when you are going to court will control your life after the trial too.

At first, my grief was evidenced by total shock. You cannot imagine how horrible it was. Everything was so raw. When I would hear the words "gun, murder or shoot", I would just about have a physical response. My sister said that one minute I would be crying and then the next minute I would be OK. My emotions varied from anger to depression and I was terrified to let loved ones out of my sight.

I still remember Michael leaving that night and saying, "I love you, mom." It is now extremely important, because those are the last words he said to me.

It was devastating for my husband Bill because he was very close to Michael. He did not take care of himself afterwards. He carried tremendous guilt; not for any specific reason relating to the events of that night, but just because it was natural in a situation like that.

Jason was supposed to start classes on the day of Michael's funeral. The murder wiped him out for a year. He started a landscaping business with a friend, and I believe the physical activity of mowing lawns helped him. He felt unbelievable guilt over it all because the brothers had had an argument before Michael left that night. Jason had a dream two or three weeks later and in it Michael said, "I can only stay here a little while." In the dream, Jason replied, "I am sorry." Michael laughed and answered, "Well you should be, because I've always known that you loved me."

Jason now works as an information systems manager for a large corporation and as an Information Technology specialist. It is good to see him now married to a wonderful girl, settled and happy. He went through so much.

People meant well by saying things that they thought would make me feel better like, "It is God's will" or "God will never give you anything you cannot handle." But I didn't like hearing that because it put God into the equation, as if he had something to do with it.

About a year later, people were expecting me to be OK, and I thought I should be, too. I was at a very low point and starting to wonder what was wrong with me. I was reading a lot at the time and, even though I can't remember what was written, it was helpful. It took a long time to laugh again. I remember seeing a musical comedy in New York and sitting in the audience with tears rolling down my face — yet I was not even thinking about anything sad. With small steps I was finally able to allow myself to live again.

It is something you never get over. Some people just crash and burn. It helped having other families who had been in similar situations telling us we were not crazy. They helped to pull me through it. Everything shifts because your old friends do not know what to do with you or how to relate. You end up changing friends, which is a very common experience.

I helped start a chapter for Parents with Murdered Children, and we now have helped 300-350 families. Support groups are not for everyone. But it is very tough for parents who have lost children to solve things alone.

Bill and I divorced in 1997, which is also typical when a couple is confronted with such a tragedy. I really became depressed after my marriage broke up. It felt like I had lost everything and it hit me that I did not want to start over at that age. I remember the day when one of the ladies from the support group came to the door and said, "You have to get dressed and get out of bed and get going." I needed to hear those words even though I did not want to move.

I have always been spiritual, but after Michael died I struggled with my faith. I eventually came to terms with it and accepted that his death had nothing to do with God. I went through a period of awakened spirituality and started to really think of what is on the other side of death. My faith is stronger now. I have come to accept that as long as we are allowed to make our own choices, we must sometimes live with the choices of others.

If you are in a difficult situation you should ensure that you talk to someone so that you are not alone. It is necessary, as it is too tough to bottle things up. Get help from family and friends, or from an organization or a church.

Like it or not, this tragic event became incorporated into my life. I know there is evil in this world, but there is also a lot of love, compassion, and friendship. We tend to see the negative side of things but there is also the positive side of people, especially shown in those who are there for you.

Once you have gone through a tragedy, no matter what happens, you know you will survive. I am now starting to feel good about life. I am really looking forward to being a grandmother some day.

****

Brenda now devotes her time to helping other parents who find themselves in a similar situation. She works with Fight Crime: Invest in Kids, an anti-crime organization in Washington D.C., and also Healing Hearts for Families, a non-profit group that offers emotional support and information to the families and friends of those who have been killed.

CHAPTER FIVE

CHUCK NEGRON

I was living a fantasy life that seems unreal to all except those who have lived it.

****

Chuck Negron was one of the three lead singers of Three Dog Night, which, in the early part of the seventies, was one of the top rock 'n' roll acts in the world, releasing twelve consecutive gold albums.

His voice is still continually heard today as the lead singer on songs such as One, Joy to the World *(the band's most recognized hit),* Easy to Be Hard *and* Old Fashioned Love Song. *Countless other hits were recorded in the short period from 1968 to 1975, before the band broke up in 1976.*

****

I was born on June 8, 1942, five minutes before my twin sister Nancy. We grew up in the Bronx, and when I was not quite four years old, my father left us.[1] I was shy, and hated school, and by second grade I was skipping school every day.[2] My mother and sister were both wonderful to me, but my mother was around very little when I was growing up,

as she was busy working hard to pay the bills. Abandon-
ment and low self-esteem marked my childhood.

Fortunately, I discovered a natural ability to play basketball
and the success that came with that gave me some
confidence. By my senior year, I was an All-City selection
for the Bronx, and played pickup games against top players
throughout the city.[3]

I also had my first taste of singing as part of a five man a
cappella group called the Rondells.[4] We were good enough
to sing at the Apollo Theatre in Harlem on Amateur night
and did some small gigs in bars and clubs.[5]

I was offered several basketball scholarships for college and
chose to move to the West Coast and play at Hancock,
a junior college in Santa Maria, California. One of the
reasons I wanted to move to a California school was to get
to know my father better because he lived in the area.[6] He
attended many of my games and we had dinner every Friday
night, which helped to reestablish our bond.[7]

At college, I met two brothers, Paul and Dean Sorenson, in
a first semester choir class. I joined a band they had with
their two other brothers.[8] We had a few singles recorded,
one of which became a big hit in the local area. Columbia
Records auditioned our group, and they offered me, but not
the group, a recording contract.[9] The contract went nowhere, and I was let out of it.[10]

I met Danny Hutton at a party in 1965, and two years later,
he and Cory Wells asked me to join them and form a band
which became Three Dog Night. In 1968, after doing many
live shows that were well received, Dunhill Records took
notice, and signed us to a contract.

It was a wonderful, exciting time. The 60s were uncharted water. As children of the fifties, like many people our age, we were against booze because we had seen what it could do to people, so drugs seemed like a safe answer to our naive minds. But the drugs had a regressive effect on me because they brought back the pain of my childhood.

The first drug I experienced was Romilar Cough Syrup, which I drank for two weeks straight after trying it. I then moved to LSD and other drugs, and by 1970, I was using cocaine and seconals (*downers*) at a daily pace that was far beyond what a normal person would need.[11]

At the height of the band's popularity, we became very full of ourselves. Drugs were used everyday, and women basically threw themselves at us. Wherever I went I was recognized, and doors would open. Money was readily available, and by 1971, I had anything within my financial reach. I was coming off a sixth consecutive gold album with Three Dog Night, in a year where touring revenue grossed $5,000,000.[12] I was living in a three-story, 5,000 square foot Mediterranean villa in the Hollywood Hills, had a garage full of Mercedes, and was not yet even thirty years old.[13] I was living a fantasy life that seems unreal to all except those who have lived it.

I was in a constant drugged-out stupor. One night I walked right off the side of the stage to open a concert. After picking myself off the floor, I staggered back and performed. This happened more than once.[14] Drugs were a part of everything. We were chosen to be on a float for the nationally televised 1972 Rose Bowl parade and I remember snorting coke all the way through it, while Danny Hutton virtually passed out and was propped up on the float.[15] We both had serious drug problems.

In 1970, I married Paula Servetti but the marriage was doomed to fail because I was not ready to give up having sex with other women. We lasted until 1973, and while I was on tour, I discovered she had moved half the furniture out of my dream home, and had taken custody of our two-year-old daughter.

My health started to suffer and my weight dropped thirty pounds. A few times I passed out with a cigarette and lit the sheets on fire.[16] Sex with groupies, which had been a good escape, was no longer interesting to me.[17] Drugs had taken away all of my feelings.

I switched to using heroin, a habit that eventually cost $2,000 per day.[18] By 1976, the band had broken up, and I was with my second wife, Julia Densmore, who was also an addict. We had a child, Chuck III, who at birth was addicted to heroin and methadone.[19]

My habit was supported by royalty checks from Three Dog Night, and the selling of every possession I had. For a few years, I lived in seclusion with my wife, doing all the drugs I could get my hands on, despite having friends die of overdoses. In 1981, a house that we frequented almost every night, where people dropped in and did heroin, was the scene of a four-person murder by intruders. By pure chance we had not gone over that night.[20] Other close calls occurred with dealers who we owed money to. They shot at my house, and, in one case, broke in and tried to collect.[21]

My money was disappearing because of my drug habit. As well, millions had been lost by bad or questionable investments by our advisers.[22] Our house had been remortgaged, and I had sold my cars and even my prized possessions. Selling my gold records to a pawnshop for very little money was not a low; it was just a little embarrassing. I did it because I needed money fast in order to get my fix before I got on a flight.

In the spring of 1985, I entered rehabilitation. In a pattern that would continue, I did not succeed, and in December of that year, Julia left me. As well, I was terminated from the band for not living up to the condition of a contract signed for a reunion tour, which was to keep clean of drugs.[23]

Through the years, my sister, father, and mother had tried to provide all types of support for me. It got harder for them because of my lies and behavior, and eventually my mother and sister turned their backs on me.[24] I was, in all probability, going to be a lifetime junkie.

I had many lows because of the drugs: my first and second wives leaving me, realizing I was addicted and not being able to stop, and being homeless and living in an abandoned building. I lowered myself to stealing my girlfriend's jewelry as well as taking money from my daughter's wallet. I was living a life of despair, and at one point while I was living on the streets, a gang member from L. A. pointed a gun at my head, and then passed on killing me, probably because I looked like a pathetic human specimen.[25] The sadness the drugs created was overwhelming. They stole so many of my years, but yet I could not stop.

Robin, my third wife, came into my life in 1986, and she valiantly tried every possible angle to keep me clean. Finally, I ended up on the streets, living out of a paper bag. No one could tolerate me, and all family and friends had long given up. I had hepatitis C and pneumonia. I was a shell of my former self.

In September of 1991, I was put into a program called Cri-Help for one last chance at coming clean. Cri-Help was a boot camp environment that forced one to surrender. I was dying and tormented in the agony of both heroin and methadone withdrawal. I asked Mike Finnigan (*a professional musician and singer who had toured with Crosby, Stills and Nash*) for advice and he told me, "Get through this day and pray to the Lord." I remember it as the day that I did just that, and went to bed.

I had my first good sleep in months, and awoke knowing a miracle had happened! A window had opened where I had asked for just a ray of hope. I felt an empowering feeling that I could get through anything, and that feeling stayed with me through the tough elements of recovering. God blessed me with another chance.

My newfound faith allowed me to overcome the roller coaster of emotions that could change from anger to crying in just seconds. For the first time in my life, I felt profound guilt about the twenty-six years of hurt that I had inflicted on family, wives, children, fellow musicians, and friends. Drugs could no longer mask my conscience. I will never be relieved of my guilt totally, but I did make amends to several people who were so supportive to me.

I remember getting a call to help a young musician who was a junkie and could not get clean. They were telling me he was embarrassed because he knew only four or five guitar chords and had low self worth. I said I would be glad to help but no one called. A year later he was in hospital again, and I was asked once again if I would help. I repeated that I would be glad to assist. However, he later checked out of the hospital and three days later rock and roll had another high profile death. His name was Kurt Cobain, the lead singer of the band Nirvana.[26]

I have been clean for over eleven years, and I have embraced a life that I never thought I would see. My daughter Charlotte was born in December 1993, and became the first child I fathered that I truly could enjoy in a sober light. I am not a self-righteous, religious zealot. However, I do know in my heart that I am a living miracle, and that miracle is a gift from a loving and forgiving God.[27]

You don't know what you can go through until you do. You can't do it alone though, and whatever your challenge, get support. Have the ability to learn and change. Accept humility and take responsibility, and when you get through your trouble, you will have as your reward, a passion for life like you have never had. Willing to be wrong and learn again is a wonderful gift that brings back the childlike joys of life.

It's never to late to live your life.

****

Chuck is now recording and playing concerts again. His time is also given to helping other addicts in their attempts to come clean. His marriage to Robin ended in 2000 and he has since remarried Kate Vernon, an actress. In 2001 they had a daughter, Annabelle.

CHAPTER SIX

NORA LOPEZ

I saw the barrel of a rifle pointing out of a car that had pulled up beside me.

****

Nora Lopez had been told she was going to have an "accident."

****

I was born in Honduras on August 14, 1955. My mother was an extremely hard working woman. She was very focused on getting us educated, even though Honduras was a country where one could easily be deprived of proper schooling. My father worked on a banana plantation while my mother started her own business and eventually developed it into a mini-market.

I met my husband, Eduardo, in 1972. He liked me but I was not very attracted to him, however, when I saw that my mother disapproved of him, I then started to like him. He was older and more serious than I was. We started dating a year later, and when he came to talk to my parents about marriage, my father said it was OK. Eduardo worked as a sailor to make money for the wedding and we were married in November 1974. I did not know about his political convictions or any trouble he had had prior to our relationship.

Eduardo had been in the army and had been involved in some type of revolt. He was put in solitary confinement for six months, and spent much of his time in a cell where he could not lie down or stand up. He was fed only bread and water.

The more he traveled, the more he questioned why other countries had healthcare and education and Honduras did not. In his mind, the things that made a human being live with dignity were health care, education, employment, and housing as well as the ability to elect and even criticize their government. Seeing how badly some people were treated probably awakened his political consciousness.

He became involved with political parties on the left. He always felt it was unjust that 2% of the population were extremely wealthy while 18% were employed but struggled to get by and the other 80% lived in complete misery and poverty. He was appalled that at least one hundred out of every thousand children died of preventable diseases. I did not have the answers to those problems or even care that much at that time. In Honduras you need more than one job to have a good living, and I worked two jobs much of the time. I thought, "Why should I worry about the rest of the world if I have three children that are an urgent responsibility?"

When the revolution in Nicaragua started, things got worse, as there was a paranoia that Communists were trying to take over. Honduras, in my opinion, was a more apathetic country politically as most people were more concerned with survival and living for the day, yet it became a strategic country for the United States during the Cold War. People who were doing things, or who were perceived to be doing things, against the government were targeted.

On August 10, 1981, Eduardo was going to school at night when he was stopped by a military car and taken away. A witness, a woman who knew me, bravely followed it and watched it stop in front of the police headquarters where she saw him taken into the building.

I waited up all night for him. At work the next day the woman came up to me and told me what happened, so I went to the police station and said I was looking for Eduardo Lopez. The policeman said, with a smirk on his face, that he did not know where he was. I had no choice but to leave and go back to work.

A co-worker told me that I should go back to the police station. He also told me what floor to look for Eduardo on. When I marched up the stairs the policeman asked me where I was going, and I told him that I was going to take food to my husband and I kept walking. I went to the floor where I had been instructed to go, and when I stuck my head through the door, I saw Eduardo in a cell in front of me. That was the proof I needed. I went to see the Captain and asked him, "Why is he there?" and "Do I need to get a lawyer?" He said they found a subversive newspaper in my husband's briefcase and that he was being held incommunicado.

I told him that the constitution says you can read anything you want to, and the Captain replied, "We tell you what to read here — go home and wait." A friend of Eduardo's, who was a journalist, advised me to somehow keep seeing him and not to leave him there over the weekend or he would likely be killed, so every day I would take him food. One day, Eduardo handed me a slip of paper, but he was so sweaty that the print had run, and the paper was unreadable.

I was angry and told the police that I would go on a hunger strike and bring in my children too. My protests and actions worked as he was released on the 14th of August, and I was made responsible for him. They told me, "Make sure he keeps his mouth shut, and does not read." They also stole his wedding band and when I asked about that they told me to go home. I found out later that the subversive newspaper that was in his briefcase was one that was handed out to all students.

At home, I saw that he had lost fifteen pounds and had marks on him from torture. It turned out that the paper he had handed me in the prison said that he was being tortured. I felt like going to that place and blowing it up and destroying those evil people. I asked him, "Don't you hate the torturer?" He replied, "No, he is a product of a cruel society and he is just doing his job."

Eduardo was even more vocal after being released and he became a vice-president on a national committee for human rights. In October of 1982, he found out that he was on a hit list, so he left for Miami. I visited him in September 1983, three months after giving birth to our third child. I realized we could offer our children nothing as illegal aliens, so I returned to Honduras, and got a letter from the committee for human rights to help support Eduardo in his bid for refugee status in the Canadian Consulate in Atlanta. It was rejected so he returned to Honduras. He said he would likely die if he came back, but despite the risk he returned because we had to be together as a family. Our children were one and a half, four, and nine years old.

In December of 1984, Eduardo was abducted for a second time. He was kidnapped on the street and there were people who saw it but they were afraid to come forward. I sent telexes to Amnesty International, the United Nations, and other media. I did not know that Amnesty International had started a campaign for Eduardo and the safety of our family, too. I also sent a letter to the U.S. Ambassador's wife. The U.S. embassy continued to tell journalists that the disappearances were just rumors. I later was given heartbreaking news from people on the inside. Eduardo had been killed in early January after being tortured.

I was told that I was going to have an "accident," as I had been making noise through the media. Once, I was driving to my home after teaching at night, and I saw the barrel of a rifle pointing out of a car that had pulled up beside me. I sped up to escape, but I think someone was looking out for me because a second car came between us and stayed there for a while. I think they may have known each other. The other car forced the one with the rifle to the side and although it was only for about three minutes, it seemed like an eternity. The "watchdog" car stayed with me until I got home. There were thousands of letters coming to the country and this is why I believe I was not killed, even though he had been.

A rich man who I had worked for, and who had liked one of my sisters, told me I had to leave and paid for my ticket to get out of the country. I left Honduras for Canada, a widow at age 29, with my three children, in June of 1985.

I went from a tropical country to a cold country. It was like walking into a freezer. I knew some English but people spoke too fast and with a different accent than I was used to, which made the language tough to learn. It was frustrating because I knew I was smart, yet some people looked at me as if I was stupid.

My first job was with a temporary service company working for two days as a receptionist typing invoices. They liked me at the agency and sent me to work the night shift for five months at Bell Canada. This gave me a lot of confidence.

I did not want my children to feel that they had been left with someone who could not take care of them, and I also wanted them to feel less afraid. They were terrified that I would be abducted, and I was afraid they would be, even when we were in Canada. It took me many years to relax about this.

The congregation of a Presbyterian church in the area helped financially to support me and my children, and Amnesty International helped pay for my training in conversational English. People from these groups became my friends and teachers.

Faith and my children got me through the toughest times. I had grown up as a Catholic and every night I would pray, even though in Honduras the Catholic Church was regarded by many as having too close a tie with the government. My mother's advice was that when the load is really heavy and you cannot hold it, give it to God. We cannot explain why things happen to us. My faith kept me going in my darkest hours.

I am an optimist and I always count my blessings. For example, I can walk, see, and talk. I have my children, a new husband, and good friends that I can count on. It is important how you face your problems. We have the power to wake up in the morning and decide if that day is one we are going to view as good or miserable.

We all have power.

****

Amnesty International(AI) is a worldwide voluntary activist movement working for human rights. It does not support or oppose any government or political system and it is concerned solely with the impartial protection of human rights.

AI's mission is to undertake research and action that will prevent and end abuses of individuals' rights. It has over one million members in over 140 countries and territories. It seeks the release of prisoners who have been unfairly detained because of their beliefs, ethnic origin, sex, language or other status.

Nora Lopez is now the coordinator of an immigrant and refugee health program and does front line work as a community health worker.

CHAPTER SEVEN

ROBERT GRIMMINCK

My biggest fear lay in someone finding out the secret that I had revealed only to my wife and her family.

****

Ironically, a workplace accident in 1992, that left Robert with two herniated discs, changed his life for the better by forcing him to confront his biggest fear.

****

I was born on September 15, 1956, the fourteenth child in a family of fifteen. My parents had emigrated from Holland to Canada just three years prior. We grew up in a small community outside of Chatham, Ontario. My father was a talented and versatile man whose jobs to support the family ranged from being a carpenter to a school janitor. Financially the family scraped by because the most he ever earned in one year was roughly five thousand dollars.

I was classified as a very slow learner, and because I could not communicate my thoughts to others, it was very frustrating. It led me to quit school after tenth grade. Needless to say, I also had extremely low self-confidence and self-esteem.

In 1979, I met my wife, Theresa. Within three years we were married, and she began work as a registered nurse at a local hospital. Like my family, hers was hardworking, but unlike mine, they were well educated yet they never looked down at me. We had five children, all boys, between 1982 and 1992.

I went to work for a window manufacturer, where I moved up the ladder to become a quality control coordinator. I went to great lengths to conceal my illiteracy. I even managed to provide reports to my supervisor by buying magazines, taking articles that seemed to talk about good or bad things in related products, and then substituting our product names. This was possible because some words I could recognize even though I was not able to comprehend many of the large paragraphs. Unfortunately, one day my supervisor offhandedly remarked that my writing looked like it came from a magazine. I quit that day, horrified that my secret of being illiterate, might become known.

Everything changed after a workplace accident on March 10, 1992. I tripped over a steel lid on a cement floor, and was thrown against a steel rack and fell down on my backside. I ended up with four collapsed discs and two central herniated discs. There was a lot of swelling and I lost feeling in my legs. I was bedridden for months and anytime I moved, it felt like I was being jolted with lightning.

I was left with a permanent spinal injury and was looking at being heavily medicated for the next year. I was in constant pain, and at a stage where my wife had to help me move my arms and legs. They put me on so many drugs and painkillers that it took control of my thinking. The worst part of recovering was the withdrawal from the drugs.

I felt as useless as a man could be because I was unable to help support my family. I was likely handicapped for life, and I had no job prospects that could meet my limited capabilities. My wife and children helped me through the toughest days by keeping my spirits up, and somehow I managed to avoid falling into a deep depression. My thinking was not "Poor me, I have an excuse to fail," but "How can I get back to a life that I want."

The back specialist thought it best to avoid surgery because later on I might suffer from arthritis and be in a wheelchair sooner. I was put through a lot of therapy. It took six months to walk and over a year to even feel comfortable sitting again. A simple sneeze would put me out for two weeks.

The Workman's Compensation people who counseled me encouraged me to go back to school and upgrade my education. At that time I could multiply up to five, was at a seventh grade reading level, and a fifth grade writing level.

I graduated with my high school diploma in June of 1994. It was a surreal feeling. I knew that because I had achieved this, that I could go to the next level of learning. Over the next four years, I completed a three-year industrial design program with a one-year co-op program. I was not self-conscious about going to school with students who were twenty years younger than I was and who called me "dad", because it was exciting. By listening to them, I gained so much perspective.

My confidence grew to the point where I felt that people were actually looking to me as an inspirational figure. I began focusing my energies not just on my personal recovery, but on improving the situation for others. My anger at the school system was disappearing.

In May 1993, a teacher, Wilma de Rond, had recognized that I had a learning disability, and showed me how to get around it. I was tested a few years later and I learned that my learning disability was called P300 brain stem response disorder, which affects how one hears and processes information. On the bright side, this could be worked with. It turned out that two of my children also had this disorder and were not slow learners as they had been labeled. Ironically, had I found out about the P300 limitation before I started learning again, I think it would have stopped me from progressing. I could have blamed the disorder for my illiteracy. In my case, not knowing I had this disability allowed me to exceed it.

I have a very strong belief that there is a God or a greater power, and I have become more aware of my spiritual surroundings. I believe that all people have good qualities and that you should assist those who can't help themselves but are willing to try. You should forgive those who offend you the most. Help as many people as you can and do not expect anything in return.

Many people live a generally happy life but with an underlying frustration, feeling continually trapped. They want to escape the invisible walls that imprison them, but they need inspiration and proper guidance to escape this gray zone. Don't be afraid to let your guard down and allow other people to help you.

You have to be persistent, motivated, and have a clear vision of your short and long-term goals. Do what you love. I have hit the bottom many times. In life, you are never done. You must keep trying.

Positive thinking that focused on solutions to my problems, as opposed to dwelling on the constraints, was key to my recovery. Don't fall into the trap of blaming others for your situation. Be realistic and you will achieve what you want.

You can get over any obstacle with hard work and help from others.

****

According to the National Institute for Literacy, it is estimated that twenty percent of American adults read at or below a fifth grade level.   40 million Americans over the age of sixteen have significant literary needs. A large percentage of this group are unemployed or only have a part-time job. The correlation between literacy and poverty is direct and significant.

Illiteracy creates a vicious cycle in families where one or both of the parents have not completed high school because their children are five times more likely to drop out than are the offspring of other parents.

After the accident, Robert went back to school. In one year at the Center for Adult Learning, he completed five grade levels, maintained an A average in eleven subjects, and became the valedictorian for his class of 300 graduating students. He also wrote and delivered a speech to the Royal Commission on Learning, in which he emphasized the negative effects of the lack of education that his family had experienced.

Robert went to college in London, Ontario, and won three college-wide awards, including "The Presidents Award" which was the school's highest honor. He graduated on March 17, 1997 and became president of the alumni association. He also spoke to others about literacy, conducted workshops on "Returning to Learning," and published, "To Dream A Different Dream," an autobiography that also included some of his poetry.

CHAPTER EIGHT

M'LISS and CHUCK SWITZER

The abuse started on the first night of our honeymoon, and got worse over time, culminating with Chuck taking a rifle to bed.

****

Chuck and M'Liss Switzer were married on December 29, 1962. They were both in their early twenties, and had dated for over a year.

****

PART ONE: M'LISS SWITZER

I met Chuck through a bible college. He was coming to Minnesota to be a minister. We dated for one year and then got married on December 29, 1962. On our honeymoon night he started to hit me because I did not climax when we had sex. I ran off crying to the bathroom thinking that this was the way marriage is. He came to the door and apologized. All I could do was hope and believe it would get better, because I had nowhere else to go.

I was born April 30, 1940, in St. Paul, Minnesota and was only one year old when my parents divorced. That was quite a scandal at the time. It gave our family a stigma, and as children we were somewhat shunned by other neighborhood kids. My father ran a cigar store, and I can only remember one year when he came by regularly for visits.

Mother was a homemaker, and had an easy going and likable personality. Financially, we scraped by the whole time I was growing up. I was cross-eyed and had buckteeth, which forced me to wear braces for eight years. Somehow, she organized operations for my eyes and teeth at the University of Minnesota Hospital.

Both my parents died when I was twelve years old. My father died of a heart attack and two weeks later my mom passed away after a two-year battle with cancer. My oldest sister became our legal guardian; otherwise we would have been wards of the state. I was not close to her at all because she was moody, crabby, and nine years older than myself. She also carried anger at having to look after two sisters who were so much younger.

She became abusive both physically and verbally and she was always telling me how ugly and dumb I was, and that I could not be trusted. I never fought back because the message I got from others was that she was not doing anything wrong, so I assumed I was the problem and was compliant and obedient in response. I felt I could not leave home because it would be met with strong opposition. Despite the abuse, I thought my sister was very intelligent, and it took me many years to believe that I was not stupid.

After the wedding, Chuck went away for a tour of duty. He spent fifty months in the service, of which fourteen were overseas. He didn't see our first daughter until she was four months old. I had her when I was twenty-five, our second daughter when I was twenty-six, and four years later I had our only son.

We still did family things like going on trips and we would sometimes have one month that was good. However, life got bad if he was under stress of any sort. If I ever criticized him he would beat me up so as to shut me up. Sexually, if I did not do what he wanted, he would verbally abuse me or throw me out of bed. If he had a bad day at work, or breakfast was not perfect, then I was at risk. Anything could trigger an outburst. He hit the children as a way to discipline them, but for the most part, I was the focus of his violence. I never fought back because I figured I would just make it worse.

The violence also got more intense and frequent as years went by. The worst beating I had was with a webbed military belt that left welts all over my body. This beating occurred because I had told Chuck that a motor scooter he had lent to a friend, in my opinion, might break down or cause an accident. He reacted the way he always did when I was critical: I was beaten with fists, kicked, and shoved. I feared that he might kill me, intentionally or unintentionally, when he had the belt around my neck.

The members of our church, family, and friends would not approach Chuck, probably because they never believed the abuse to be serious or because they felt uncomfortable. When I told people that he had been hitting me, I felt that they looked at me in a way that said, "What are you doing wrong?"

During one violent incident, I managed to get away from Chuck and I spent the night in the car. I then went to the police station and eventually found a sensitive officer who helped me. I finally charged Chuck with assault in January

1982. I did not know then, that I could get an order for protection. The system is vastly improved today.

When I charged him with assault, I was prepared and had friends with me for support. Chuck panicked when he was told, and said he was leaving and he was not going to give me a dime. He broke our credit cards into pieces and told our oldest daughter he was never coming back. He ended up not leaving, which was the worst of all situations because that is when abusive men are most desperate. The night before we went to court he brought a loaded Winchester rifle to bed and threatened to commit suicide. I managed to quietly reassure him that things would work out OK.

The law was the only force big enough to get him to stop after twenty years of violence. He pleaded guilty and went for treatment. After the trial he had one more violent episode, so I got a court order, which forced him to move out. After that, there was no violence. He learned to take time-outs when I would ask him if his anger was escalating.

I discovered that there was help for the victim, too. Once I learned it existed, nothing could keep me away from getting assistance. Our children went through programs for adolescent groups, and I served on the Board of Directors for the Domestic Abuse Project from 1991-2000. I am proud of the accomplishment of going from client to board member.

When I look back on our dating, I realize that Chuck's admission of hitting his mother should have sent up a red flag in my mind. The only other sign of potential abuse before marriage was his anger, which he showed by throwing things, kicking vehicles, and other ways of displaying rage. When I said, "I do," I believe that in Chuck's mind, I became his property and he had every right to abuse me.

People wonder why I waited so long before leaving. The first challenge would be getting help after the phone had been pulled out of the socket, or trying to leave when he had taken my car keys. Where would I go when I walked out the door? I had three children. Should I take them with me or leave them with him? I had no family to go back to, and neither the energy nor strength to deal with the welfare system.

Looking back, I know it was my spirituality and belief in God that carried me through everything.

My advice to women who are being emotionally or physically abused is to get the appropriate help. By appropriate help, I mean a specialist in domestic violence. Do not think it is only your partner who needs help, and that when they get it, the problem will be eliminated. You need help, too, to feel better about the situation, and to deal with any issues you may have.

****

PART TWO: CHUCK SWITZER

It has been close to twenty years since I went to bed with a Winchester rifle, contemplating suicide.

I was born on January 14, 1943 in Leadville, Colorado. My father was a contractor and farmer and was away a lot. My mother had four children to raise and she also had to manage three hundred acres of farmland plus do chores such as milking thirty cows.

My parents had a violent relationship from day one. There was always conflict when they were together, and physical violence occurred at least once a month. My father and my mother never solved the domestic violence, and they eventually divorced.

I was never taught that violence is inappropriate. I had never been a brawler; all my issues were with my wife and children. Things as simple as getting lost while driving often led to trouble. When I was violent, I felt blind rage. It was mainly about power and an effort to gain control over M'liss or the children. Sometimes it was to turn off her anger. It was my way of getting to an agreement without negotiation. After abusive episodes with M'liss, I felt guilt, and was sometimes suicidal.

I only stopped because I was motivated by a fear of the law. To break the cycle, I needed therapy. I had to visualize myself as non-violent. It is possible that an episode could happen again. The best way to describe my battle to avoid a relapse into violence is that I have a wolf in my face and I am hanging onto its ears. Whether he will bite me depends on my grip. I am getting older now, but so is the wolf, yet I must keep my grip strong all the time. If I feel my control is slipping then I need to do something about it right then and there. The only way it could happen again is if I miss the warning signs that precede violence.

The relationship with our children today is pretty near excellent. I can now play the role of father and grandfather and show support and approval.

The perpetrator of the violence must take responsibility for it and be ready to change, while the victim has to be ready to forgive. Our story is a success because we stopped the abuse, NOT simply because the relationship was saved.

****

Chuck and M'Liss are now living a peaceful life together. Their story is very unusual, because it is rare for a marriage to survive the cycle of abuse.

Domestic Violence almost never ends by itself. It usually escalates until it culminates in either separation or the death of the victim. Victims often stay in abusive relationships because they feel they have no place to go, doubt their ability to support themselves, fear their abuser will kill them if they leave, or believe that they don't deserve happiness.

The best solution is the one that stops the violence. In most situations, the only way for this to happen is for the victim to leave the marriage immediately and permanently without attempting to achieve reconciliation.

CHAPTER NINE

JOHN HILLER

I sat down at the table and lit a cigarette. Suddenly, it felt as if someone was sitting on my chest.

****

In 1970, John Hiller's baseball career was suddenly interrupted. He signed a professional baseball contract with the Detroit Tiger organization at age nineteen. John spent four years in the minors before cracking the big league roster. His team, the Detroit Tigers, reached the pinnacle of success when they won the 1968 World Series over the St. Louis Cardinals in seven games.

****

I was a hard worker and I had never consumed alcohol before I went into pro ball, but playing in New York State at age 19, I got an early education in having fun. I had a blast my first three years being single and hanging out with guys who liked to have a good time. It was probably very similar to college life, because we were all broke and having fun. I was always sad when the season ended because I was having such a good time. In the offseason I went back home to Ontario to work with my Dad at his small body shop. I did nothing towards advancing an alternate career, or conditioning. Basically I just waited for spring training to arrive.

In the summer of 1964, I met my future wife at the ballpark in Duluth, Minnesota and we married in September, 1965. My road to the majors started in Jamestown, and went through Duluth, Knoxville, Montgomery, Syracuse, and Toledo before I finally got to Detroit. I had the honor of pitching in the World Series in 1968, although I wished I had done better. Nonetheless, it was great winning the World Series.

By 1971, I weighed 215 pounds, which was for me about thirty pounds overweight, and was smoking two packs of Marlboro "high test" cigarettes per day. I was living in Northern Minnesota, and on January 11, I had just gotten back from a snowmobile trip. I lit a cigarette and was having a coffee when I experienced pain running down each arm, as well as high on the shoulder and through the neck.

I grabbed my chest. At first, I thought I was having lung problems. It hurt more each time I inhaled the cigarette. So in my anger, I grabbed the package and nailed it to the rafters in the basement because I knew there was some relation between the cigarettes and the pain I was feeling.

After my third incident in an hour, I called the doctor and he said to come into the hospital. I was huffing, puffing, and sweating like crazy as I unhitched the snowmobile to get there. At the hospital, they took one look at me and put me flat on my back for three weeks. I had had a heart attack at age 27. The problem was at the back of the heart and two arteries were blocked. Although my cholesterol was high, I had no family history of heart disease. It made no sense as to why this happened to me.

The three weeks of complete bedrest had me going bananas. An internist told me I would not be able to pitch for the 1971 season, so I called the General Manager of the Tigers, Jim Campbell, and told him that I had a heart attack. He started to laugh, thinking I was bullshitting him.

After the heart attack I was not too depressed, probably because I am a pretty laid back person. I am never too up or too down, sort of like a typical Canadian fan, who when watching a sports event, doesn't yell or stand up but just sits and applauds.

The hospital put me on a diet and I quit smoking. I decided to have an experimental surgery called a partial illial bypass. Studies of young people had shown this procedure could reverse heart disease. I would be a test patient. With no education or skills and two kids, I needed income. This option offered some hope that I might be able to pitch again.

I weighed 145 pounds when I was discharged and I could not even walk two blocks because the muscles in my legs had atrophied. I tried to play some golf and got in 1½ holes before my brother-in-law had to carry me home.

I was fortunate that two brothers who owned a department store, Monty and Irwin Goldfine, let me work for them selling furniture. At the time, I had such little strength that I would get tired moving a cushion. They let me leave at any time in the day to go to the Y and work out. I slowly started to get myself back in shape.

There was no follow-up from the Tiger organization, and no physical therapist to help me. After a couple of months, I drew a square on the concrete wall in the basement of the Y and started to pitch a baseball at it. At first it was very soft tossing, because my muscles were weak. By late summer and fall, I started to "pop" the ball again. At that point, I thought I could return to playing pro baseball.

By Nov 7, I could run two miles, and I weighed 165 pounds. My cholesterol was down, one artery was totally clear, and the other only blocked 5%. The doctor said, "OK, you are free to go!" I called the Tigers and they were uninterested. I thought they would be a little more excited, but the problem was the Lions (*Detroit's football team*) had lost a player, Charley Hughes, that year on the field to a heart attack so they were a little gun-shy. As well, both the University of Michigan Hospital and Henry Ford Hospital would not endorse me coming back since they were concerned about the stress of me pitching in pressure situations.

I got an appointment with Dr. Willis Hurst, who was former President Lyndon Johnson's personal physician. I spent the entire day with Dr. Hurst and his staff doing tests and having them check my mental status. His advice to the Tigers was, "If John Hiller does not get back into baseball he will have a heart attack."

Meanwhile Billy Martin (*the Detroit Tiger manager*) had been bugging management to get me back. Knowing Martin, he would have thought it was the best way to die if I was to have a heart attack on the baseball diamond. Shortly after that, they told me to join them in Chicago. They got Les Cain, who had arm trouble at the time, and had both of us pitch in the bullpen side by side. They would pick one of us for the only spot open on the roster. I knew he had no chance, because after all I had been through I was determined that I would not be beaten.

My favorite memory is the night I came back. The first hitter was Dick Allen of the Chicago White Sox, one of the top power hitters of that era. I threw a first pitch curve and a second pitch fastball, both for strikes, but he did not swing at either pitch. It was as if he was saying, "If that is all you have, then bring it." So I did, and he almost hit it off the top of the roof at Comiskey Park. A homerun to the first batter I faced after 1½ years on the disabled list. Welcome back to the Majors! I was in a fog that night but just being back pitching made it wonderful despite the homerun I had given up.

I was throwing better than I ever had. I felt no pressure late in a game because I had a different perspective on life. I now understood that the game was important to my career but not to my life. In the mid 70s, I changed all that I did, and for five years, I did not smoke or drink and stayed on my diet.

Sitting around in the bullpen was fun and we joked around most of the time. We played cards, and for a while we had a portable television and a cassette player out there. We also had binoculars and telescopes to check out girls in the stadium. In Baltimore, where there was a lot of room, we would take our bats and balls, put a few holes in the ground and play a golf-like game out there.

Ultimately, I understood where my talents had come from and I eventually became a baseball chapel leader. I did not publicly announce my faith at first, as I wanted to wait until things were going well, so people would not think I was just using religion as a crutch. I did not let success change anything.

In 1980, I felt I had lost a little on my pitches and I was having some arm trouble too. At age 38, I did not feel I would rebound. I may have retired prematurely but I did not want to embarrass myself. I sold insurance for a month, worked in Florida for a little bit, and ran a one-man pet store where I had fun but never made any money, since I gave all the pets free to little kids and pretty women. I have never really adjusted to being out of baseball. Like 99% of ex-players, I miss the camaraderie, and when I go to do fantasy camps (*where retired players instruct and play baseball with paying fans*) for the Tigers in Florida, I turn into a big kid again once I put on the uniform.

I owe my recovery to a number of people. The understanding and assistance of the Goldfines played a big part in helping me get back to a position where I could pitch again and I will be forever grateful for their help. The Tiger team physician, Dr. Livingood, was always in my corner, and my wife was very supportive too. My father was a man of few words, but when he said something it was important. I will always remember the confidence it gave me when my father said, "You will be back in baseball and I know you will be better than ever."

I do not view myself as courageous, because I knew I had to play baseball to make a living. Many people said I could not do it, but that pissed me off and made me more determined, so that I focused on proving them all wrong.

Don't let anyone change your dreams regardless of what the circumstances are. It will be if it is meant to be, and if it is not then something else will take its place.

****

John won the American League Fireman of the Year (awarded to the top relief pitcher in his league) in 1973 when he posted a 1.44 earned run average and appeared in 65 games. He pitched until 1980 for the Detroit Tigers, is a member of the all-time Tiger team, and is also an inductee of the Canadian Baseball Hall of Fame.

CHAPTER TEN

GERALDINE FERRARO

I was told, "Gerry, I hope you are serious, because you are taking a man's place you know."

****

Geraldine Ferraro made history as the first woman to contend for Vice President of the United States. She and Presidential hopeful Walter Mondale challenged incumbent President Ronald Reagan and Vice President George Bush for the 1984 election.

After devoting thirteen years to raising three children, Geraldine reentered the workforce full-time. She was elected in 1979 to the House of Representatives and was instrumental in creating legislation that helped provide financial equity for women. She had first hand knowledge of pay inequities because only two years earlier she was earning less than her male counterparts despite doing the same job.

During the 1984 campaign, Geraldine and her husband were the focus of zealous and unrelenting media attacks. The election was a landslide for Reagan, as he won 49 of the 50 states.

****

My father was an Italian immigrant. He and my mother ran a restaurant, bar, and general store in Newburgh, New York. When I was eight years old, my father passed away, and because he had no life insurance, my mother was forced to sell our house and move my brother and me back to New York City and into a small apartment in South Bronx.[1] She went out to work as a crochet beader—a skill she had learned as a child. She sacrificed to provide us with the best education.

I started law school in 1956. I think there were three, maybe four, women in the program when I started. I was in the evening class, as I taught school during the day. When I applied to law school, I was told, "Gerry, I hope you are serious, because you are taking a man's place, you know." At that time, you could discriminate against females and not admit the most qualified candidate, as doing so was not against the law.

One of the reasons there were so few women was because most were not interested in pursuing a legal career. Not only was it difficult to be admitted to law school, but at that time, many girls were more focused on getting their "MRS." degree along with a bachelor's degree, and in fact, many had engagement rings at graduation.

Most professors treated us the same as they did everyone else, although I recall one who never gave a woman a good mark no matter how smart she was. After the first year, we were given student numbers, and marks changed significantly for females, because the instructor could no longer tell it was a she who wrote the paper. One other professor would call on a woman only if it was an embarrassing topic being discussed but any hostility that existed was from a very small number of teachers and staff.

I had a difficult time getting a job on graduation from law school in 1960, even though I finished in the top ten percent. At one firm I was interviewed five times. The fifth interview was with a senior partner. He proceeded to tell me how terrific I was and I thought I had the job. He then told me that they were not hiring any women that year. I was absolutely livid. I stood up and said, "You have just spent 45 minutes of my time telling me how terrific I am — well, my mother tells me that every morning," and I stormed out.

I applied to the District Attorney's office in Manhattan, went through several interviews and was offered a position. When I told them I was getting married in September, they withdrew the offer because they said, "You will not be able to fulfill the three-year commitment because you are Catholic and will probably have a baby right away and leave." That was the type of thing that could be said in 1960. Many firms already had a woman on staff, so they were more comfortable rejecting a female, as they already had their quota.

I realized I couldn't do anything about it. I would say to myself that these are terrible people and then move on. Fortunately, a law has been passed which makes this type of discrimination illegal and such a firm would now find themselves in court.

In 1974, I returned to the workforce and went to work in the District Attorney's Office in Queens. I started a bureau that dealt with all the sex crimes in the county, as well as with violent crimes against senior citizens, with child abuse, and with domestic violence. I called it "The Special Victims Unit."

We only had one shelter for abused women in Brooklyn that was supposed to cover Queens and Brooklyn: roughly 5.5

million people. It was very frustrating seeing women and children abused by spouses and not having a place to send them for safe haven. I would go to court to try to get a woman a court order for protection and sometimes it would work but frequently it would not.

In one case, a baby was burned badly by the mother's boyfriend and she ended up marrying him so that she could not be compelled to testify against him. I dealt with these cases only because I had to. The cases stayed with me and eventually I left the job because it was difficult to deal with emotionally. I then went where I thought I could make a difference and change some of the rules, and that is why I chose to run for Congress.

Being nominated on July 19, 1984 as the candidate for Vice President of the United States was thrilling. The night was a tremendous high, and I sincerely felt we could win the election.

The excitement was short-lived. For the next month, my ethics and my husband's were questioned. My decision not to disclose his finances (*roughly twenty other members of Congress took this approach yearly*), innuendoes about several of his real estate transactions, and a growing focus on our tax returns, clouded the political issues that we wanted to discuss with the American public.

It was emotionally exhausting. I wanted to put my arms around my family and say, "I am sorry for putting you in a position like this," and hold them so they would not hurt. I wanted to get back at the terrible people who were saying or doing these things, but unfortunately when you are a candidate, it is damn near impossible to do so. It was horrendous to read lies and twisted facts. During the course of the campaign, critics would repeat lies, as they were under no obligation to write what I said. I had to let it go, and let the story die, and a little piece of me died with it each time too.

There was one night in the campaign when I had never seen my husband so mentally beat up. I was terrified that something might happen—you never know. I got down on my knees and prayed that night, "God, please help us; help us get through this." The next day, John's voice was much better and he said, "We have been through a lot and we are going to get through this too."[2] Faith has always played a strong role in my life.

It was wonderful traveling around the country and going from event to event. I spoke to people from every walk of life. My children, who had been extremely shy, all blossomed. My son John went campaigning to something like 42 states and my two daughters were also active. Donna, my oldest, traveled all over the country. I remember my youngest daughter, Laura, getting up in front of twenty to thirty thousand people her age at a college and calmly doing a five-minute speech introducing me. This confidence has reflected itself in their lives since the campaign.

We knew at the beginning that President Ronald Reagan was extremely popular. To get rid of an incumbent you need reasons. We thought we provided many but the public liked him. I liked him, too; I just did not think he was a very good President, but evidently I was in the minority.

There was no huge depression after the election. Throughout the campaign, I felt pressure not to embarrass the women of the country and I feel we did just fine in this regard. I believe the campaign accomplished one thing that needed to be done, and that was to take the "Men only" sign down from the door of the White House.

Three years ago, I was diagnosed with an illness and I was told that the prognosis is usually three to five years to live. My first reaction was, "Thank God it's me and not my kids." I then turned around and asked, "Why is this happening?" My reaction was to try to figure out what could be done to fight it.

I am lucky that I was diagnosed early. I have been taking thalidomide and doing all the things I am supposed to do. I have wonderful doctors and the drugs are working. I feel great and expect to live to be a much older lady.

I am a believer in positive thinking. I prefer to think of the glass as half full. I think it is the best way to face life and deal with problems and adversity.

It is like breaking a glass. You will do everything you can to prevent that glass from falling off the countertop and breaking. In the process of it falling you will try to catch it, but if it hits the floor and splinters into pieces there is nothing you can do about it. Clean it up and move on. Don't stew about it. Tough times don't last. They will pass.

****

Geraldine Ferraro is fighting multiple myeloma—a condition in which cancerous plasma cells infiltrate the bone marrow and destroy bone.

CHAPTER ELEVEN

MITCH BERGER

I had been released or put on waivers five times in two years.

****

Mitch Berger is a Canadian-born football player who had a dream of playing in the National Football League (NFL). He was drafted by the Philadelphia Eagles in the sixth round of the 1994 draft—one of only two punters chosen in the league that year.

He was released by the Eagles, and failed to gain employment with several other teams that gave him tryouts. By the end of 1995, Mitch had been rejected by five teams in two years. He returned home and began to work at a gas station.

****

I was born in Kamloops, British Columbia on June 24, 1972, and was the youngest in a family of five. I started to kick at age six, instructed by my father, from a book on how to kick. He encouraged and taught me the finer aspects of sport. From age thirteen on, I went to a kicking camp in the United States each summer to upgrade my skills as a football punter and field goal kicker.

I was not drafted by any U.S. college or university. Fortunately a coach from one of the kicking camps I attended recommended I go to Tyler Junior College in Texas. Tyler was mainly a college for players who were trying to upgrade their academic qualifications to play at major universities. I was a skinny 6'4" when I went away to Tyler. It was a culture shock to be attending a school far away from British Columbia and one where, as a white player, I was a minority.

It was intimidating and very lonely. I was once bullied into buying liquor for a 6'10" basketball player. I started off my first practice by shanking (*ball goes more sideways than forward*) my first seven punts into the bleachers. Players came up to me and insulted my ability with lines like, "They brought you from Canada to kick?" It was very tough on my confidence, and I can remember initially literally crying myself to sleep.

As the year progressed, I started to feel more comfortable in my surroundings. My performance improved as I started to make friends and develop better relationships with my teammates. I ended the year as an Honorable Mention All-American kicker who both punted and kicked field goals. I had conquered my first major challenge, and my confidence in my ability had returned.

After my first year, I transferred from Tyler College to Boulder, Colorado where I joined the defending national champion, the University of Colorado Buffaloes. Initially I had the same self-doubts and uneasiness with my surroundings because I was starting for such a prestigious school. My performance improved as my comfort level increased, and over the years, I did well enough to be a First Team All-American.

The Philadelphia Eagles drafted me, but they released me after only five regular season games despite the fact I had performed decently, having eight of twenty-five punts pin the opposition inside their twenty-yard line. I joined the Cincinnati Bengals, where I was on their practice squad, which is a group of players who cling to the slim hope that they can get another chance at pro ball. I lived on the couch at the video camera coach's house, and my life consisted of watching television or going out to movies by myself. It was a very difficult adjustment, for I thrive on friends and family. Only my belief in my strong kicking leg kept me going through this period.

My performances in practice were solid, and Cincinnati wanted me to join the practice squad again, but I knew I would not get the chance to start, so I did not sign with them. I continued west, and ended up signing with the Chicago Bears in March 1995. I kicked well again, but never got a true chance at the job, as the Bears had drafted Todd Saurbrun in the second round, and he was going to be their kicker of the future. It was very frustrating, because I knew if I could get a true chance, I could play well in the NFL. I had always believed in timing, which helped me to get through this, as I was convinced someone would give me a shot. I asked for my release from the Bears, and was claimed off waivers by the Indianapolis Colts. In training camp I performed well, but again, I was frustrated when they chose to release me prior to the season.

Out of the blue, Green Bay called. They needed a kicker for their next game, and said if I kicked all touchbacks, that the job was mine. I kicked a couple, but one kick was not a touchback. I was cut the next day.

I returned home to stay with my parents. It was the fall of 1995, and no teams were expressing interest in me. Each day I would work the 6-10 a.m. shift at a friend's gas station, enduring jabs and taunts from people who knew me as the "big star" who had crashed down to earth. Even one former football coach worked me over. I used the barbs to fuel my fire, not that it needed much help. Even though all looked very bleak, I went out after work and practiced with my father who would snap balls at me to kick. I would lift weights to round out the day. Having a very supportive family that always welcomed me helped make this tough time in my life easier.

Back to Chicago I went, and again I found myself released by the Bears. They would not give me a chance to be their kicker of the future. I never gave up believing in my ability. As well, I never doubted that my chance would come, and I knew if a team gave me a good look, they would see I could perform. I was to receive one more chance.

In 1996, the Minnesota Vikings were looking for a kicker. I felt welcomed by the special teams Coach Gary Zauner, despite the scout's word on me that I was inconsistent and the fact that management gave me no chance. I found comfort in my surroundings, and this helped my performance. I finally had made a team, and was getting the chance to prove myself.

Achieving my dream was not luck, but serious persistence and continual practice. I had to swallow my pride many times. The only sure way not to succeed is to stop going for your goal. You have to believe in yourself and your talent, but ensure your assessment of your ability is correct by listening to the people whose opinions you can trust. It is this philosophy that allowed me to survive such a long period, when every door seemed closed.

Never quit going for your goal!

****

The Minnesota Vikings gave Mitch Berger what might have been his last pro tryout in 1996.   He made the team and by 1998, he had established a new NFL mark for 40 touchbacks on 114 kickoffs, smashing the prior record. That year and the next, Mitch set records and firmly established himself as one of the league's best, which was capped off by his being named to the Pro Bowl (football's All-Star game).

Mitch now plays for the New Orleans Saints.

CHAPTER TWELVE

JASON WEBER

When I opened the door there was a guy holding a gun. In Spanish, he said that he was a guerrilla and told me to come with him.

****

Jason Weber's job is to keep helicopters in working order. He works for a heavy-lift Oregon-based helicopter company, Erickson Air-Crane. On October 12, 2000, Jason and seven others were working in Ecuador near the Colombian border.

****

After graduating from high school, I spent five years in the military, and was in Somalia for both the start and end of the operation there. I met my wife at the end of 1992, while stationed in Southern California. We were married two years later and we have two daughters, born in 1996 and 1999.

When I got out of the military, I was not sure what I wanted to do. I took the first job offered to me, which was with Erickson Air-Crane, so my wife and I moved to Oregon. I started in an engine overhaul shop and moved to working exclusively on helicopters. If the helicopters are leased to a firm for an oil rig move, my job is to keep them in working order. I am away from home roughly six months of the year. It has been great to see places like Malaysia, Southern Mexico, Canada, and Ecuador.

In the fall of 2000, I went to work east of Quito, Ecuador, at the Pompeya oil drilling camp, which is almost in the Amazon jungle. The best way to describe a jungle is that it smells rotten and is eerie. If the moon is not up, it is pitch black. There is no light because you are under two hundred-foot trees. You never see the sky in the daytime and it is always either hot or raining or both.

You might see a few snakes, but mostly animals avoid you. Unfortunately, insects and ants do not stay away from you. The ants are in swarms of millions, and you have to move your stuff continually and not let it touch the ground. They come in such big armies that they will eat your clothes because they are attracted to the sweat. We would cut down a couple of small trees so we could hang hammocks on them, and then put bags on little sticks so the ants could not get to them.

On October 12, around 4:00-4:30 in the morning, I heard noises that went on for about thirty minutes. I was under the assumption that maybe someone was bringing in food since there was not a lot of screaming or yelling. Then there was a knock on the door of the building we were staying in, and when I opened it there was a guy holding a gun. In Spanish he said that he was a guerrilla and he told me to come with him.

There were about ten to fifteen heavily armed guerrillas, and they took us forty-five minutes away by helicopter. When we landed, we were marched for five days through the jungle by the guerrillas, who now numbered thirty-five to forty, stopping only briefly to rest.

My first reaction was that it seemed unreal. I did not know what to think because I was confused and did not know what was going to happen next. The only time I had ever seen anything like this was in a movie. I thought that it would only last two weeks and that I should just go with the flow. I guess I was pretty naive, because I was more pissed off at the situation than scared. They could have shot me, there was no doubt about it, and they would have if I had tried to run. I felt I could have escaped, but I did not try because it would have been bad for the other seven hostages.

As a prisoner, I found it tough to just sit in one spot and not talk or do anything. I started doing pushups or hanging on a branch just to pass the time. Everybody coped using different methods. I thought of a million ways I would like to kill the S.O.B.s, and my boss and friend Steve probably thought about it more and had a billion ways.

At one point we were given a chessboard, which gave us something to do, and Steve and I would play one game for three hours. They kept us on the move every ten to twenty days. We would be on the road for ten days straight sleeping at a different point every night.

Coincidentally, another hostage named Ron Sander had grown up in Oklahoma as well, and we talked a lot. I did not trust a couple of my fellow prisoners because I felt they did not have a lot of respect for people and that it was all about them. I wasn't fluent in Spanish, but could understand it reasonably well, and heard one of the hostages that I did not trust talking to the guerrillas about me and my family. He never should have been doing this, for the guerrillas had no reason to know about me. This happened just before Ron Sander was freed and it makes me wonder now if something the one hostage said led to Ron being picked.

One of the toughest parts of the ordeal was that I did not know what my family had been told or if they were being looked after. I just wanted twenty seconds to tell them, "I am fine, don't worry about me, we are going to get through this so you just take care of home and keep things straight and the family going." We were all worried, but I started to realize my family would be looked after if something went wrong, so I just focused on getting myself out of there.

There was a book I remembered reading about a kid who could contact everyone by envisioning a string going out and touching people. I knew it was silly but I would sit in my hammock and imagine what time it was back home or what my oldest daughter was up to, and try to concentrate on sending her a message because she would be old enough to understand it.

I have never been religious yet, when I was sitting down there, I would pray for a little while when I was not angry at the situation. When I was angry, I felt that if there was a God, there was no reason for any of us to be punished like that.

We were fed cans of what could best be described as cat food. Another time, they beat a sloth slowly to death for fun, and then the next thing we knew we were eating it for dinner. We also ate really small fish, head, guts and all, as well as "rat-like" rodents.

I always set deadlines, and decided that if after three months things were not positive, then I would try to think about how to get out of there. At the three month mark, negotiations with the kidnappers and the authorities were going OK. They came and told us they were going to send someone home, and Ron Sander was chosen. They said he was selected because at age 54, he was the oldest American there.

At the four-and-a-half month mark it seemed more positive as our captors said we would be home in eight days, which then turned into twenty days. I was starting to snap and was at my breaking point. They kept making different excuses and I just wanted to start ripping things apart.

Shortly after that, they released us. It took four to five hours to walk to the closest town. I didn't believe it when the villagers told us that Ron Sander had been killed, but when we got to the military base we found out that it was indeed the truth. I did not even know how to react. We had assumed that he had been freed in good faith. I will never forget Ron or think of him without getting a tear in my eye. He was one of the most decent men I have ever known.

We didn't believe we were free until we got on the plane for the flight home. I started to relax when we got going on the runway, and my only worry then was how my family would receive me.

When I first returned to Oregon, I would sit out on the deck, and stare at the sky. It was nice to be able to see it after being in the jungle for so long, and not to have to worry. I was 215 pounds when I was kidnapped, and when I returned I was only 175 pounds. At first, I was so confused. I found myself pacing in the house, standing in the pantry staring at the walls, wondering what I came out to do. I had no nightmares, but I was very angry, and at work I was prone to snapping really quickly. My company had given us a day off for every day we were in the jungle, but I chose to stay away from work for only two months because I found it tough not to be working.

I am still just as hardheaded as I was—maybe even more than I was before, which my friends might find hard to believe. I did some counseling and it was a relief for me to talk to someone even though no big revelation came out of it. All the guy did was listen and tell me to get a punching bag.

I look back on it now as me being in the wrong place at the wrong time. I was furious because I wished I had known more about the risks in that country. I am mad that the situation took so long to resolve and that someone had to die for me to get home.

If you are facing difficult times, try not to dwell on the situation because there is no sense worrying about the bad things that may happen. Think about the good things instead.

If something needs to be fixed, then you have to do it yourself. It boils down to depending on yourself. You can't let other people take care of you all your life.

Before the kidnapping, I would go to work, come home for a few days and then go away again. Work was always first. Now I do the same job, but nothing is done without talking with my family. I think, at the time, neither my wife nor I knew any better, because I was in the military when we started our relationship, so we were always apart for periods of time. I did not have my priorities quite in line before. I did not have my family on the level they should have been and I have found out that they are a lot more important to me than I realized.

It is sad that sometimes it takes extreme situations in life to wake you up.

****

On March 1, 2001, 141 days after being kidnapped, Jason and the other captives were released when the companies of the hostages paid a ransom of allegedly $13 million dollars. It is believed they were abducted by professional kidnappers who were from Colombia and that Ron Sander had been murdered because a ransom had not been paid by a specified date.

Jason continues to work for Erickson Air-Crane.

CHAPTER THIRTEEN

JANET GUTHRIE

I knew that being a woman was irrelevant in terms of my ability to race competitively, but no one else seemed to share that view.

****

Janet Guthrie was the first woman to compete in the Indianapolis 500 and the Daytona 500, both in 1977.

In the mid-1970s, she left her job as a technical editor and became a full-time professional racecar driver. Financially, she scraped by. Despite success in various car races, she could not find sufficient sponsorships to pay the costs associated with world class competitive racing.

An opportunity to break through the "glass ceiling" of professional oval-track auto racing came in 1976, when Rolla Vollstedt, a car builder, invited her to test one of his cars at the Ontario speedway in California. The test was a success despite the fact that she drove with a broken foot.

In 1978, at age 39, she finished ninth in the Indianapolis 500, which still stands as the best finish by a woman driver. She also posted top-ten finishes on both the NASCAR Winston Cup stock car and the Indy car circuits.

****

My family would have been called eccentric had they been rich. I was the oldest of five children. We were never made to think we must do what is conventional. There were no thoughts that the boys would go to college and the girls wouldn't. My parents gave us a very even-handed upbringing.

I always had a sense of adventure but we lived way out in the country so most of my access to excitement was through books. Reading about World War One and World War Two fighter pilots piqued my interest in flying. It became my first great adventure when I got older. I did a parachute jump when I was sixteen because I had just finished the book *Spirit of St. Louis*, and was inspired by Charles Lindbergh's account of his parachute jump.

I earned my private license to fly planes at seventeen, which was the youngest possible age you could get it at that time. I think I was about twenty years old when I got my commercial license, and my flight instructor's rating came shortly after that. Had it been possible for a woman to do at that time, I would have gone into the service to fly fighter planes.

My first flight instructor, Mary Tracy Gaffaney, was a tremendous role model. She was in her twenties then, and later became America's first world aerobatics champion. Not long ago she was still a member of the Whirly-Girls Helicopter Aerobatics team. She is 75 now and does almost 100 F.A.A. flight tests per year, and is still an F.A.A. flight examiner. Now is that a role model or what!

When I was young, I was blissfully oblivious to sexism. I must have been eighteen years old when I went to an F.A.A. seminar on some aspect of flying. The F.A.A. man saw that

I was the only woman and opened up the meeting with a joke that was so filthy that I did not even understand it until years later.

I started university, studying engineering. Out of something like 2000 students, there were eight women in the freshmen engineering class. After my freshman year I switched into physics. After graduating in 1960 with a Bachelor of Science in Physics, I worked as an engineer in the aerospace industry. I bought a Jaguar XK 120 Coupe and one thing led to another. Soon I began to compete in sports car racing. I loved it because it added the element of person-to-person competition, which I found to be a compelling combination.

After thirteen years of competing in many different races, I finally got the opportunity to drive a car at the top level. I was so thrilled because I had thought I would never get a chance. I knew that being a woman was irrelevant in terms of my ability to race competitively, but no one else seemed to share that view. I figured I could handle whatever came with the territory and took the position, "Wait and see what I can do."

The pressure was unbelievable before my first Indy car race. There were even threats of a drivers boycott. I was fortunate that the Director of Competition for the United States Auto Club, which was the sanctioning body for Indy car racing at the time, resisted those threats and gave me an opportunity to show what I could do.

A fellow driver, who had never seen me drive anything, said, "I could take a hitch-hiker and teach HIM how to drive better than Janet Guthrie." I thought that most of the stuff people said was pretty funny but some of it was certainly annoying.

I could never have done it without Rolla Vollstedt giving me a chance. He and the guys in his crew deserved the Congressional Medal of Honor for their steadfast support in the face of all the hostility at the beginning. They were really terrific. I fully appreciated what they could do with cars and they came to understand that I knew machinery, had built engines, and had been doing my own repairs for many years. We were able to form a good working relationship.

My first year on the circuit was 1976. I drove four or five races in Indy car events in Trenton, Michigan, and a few other places. The car I was driving had not been able to make the field at Indianapolis the previous year and it was marginally competitive. In my first race I qualified 15th, and felt very good about it. In the fall of 1976, we got a better car, and that is how I came to set the best time on the opening day of practice for the Indy 500 in 1977. I will never forget the moment when I took the checkered flag at the end of the four-lap qualifying run.

Drivers pay more attention to conditioning now than when I raced. You need endurance, resistance to heat, and reasonably good muscular strength. But what you really need is your mind and spirit. On the racetrack, you must have concentration, judgment, desire, and emotional detachment. Racing is a matter of spirit, not strength.

However, the best driver in the world cannot win with a car that is a "turkey." In order to win you have to have the best car or near to it. These days, it is 85% car and 15% skill of driver whereas before it was 75% car and 25% driver. At the beginning, every racer thinks they are the greatest driver ever, and of course I felt that way, too. As time went on, I started to understand the complexities of the sport, the car, the money involved, and how sponsorship is a part of it. I became more rational as to my chances. Nevertheless, I always believed I had the ability to win the races.

For women in racing, sponsorship is the biggest hurdle. That is why I was not able to continue to race. You just have to look at the evidence to see that things have not improved today. It is an outrage.

A lot of women get the feeling that in the entire history of the world, females never did anything until yesterday, and that concerns me. In my speeches, I talk about the first woman who competed in a race from Marseilles to Nice in 1898. These are the kinds of women who have always existed. During the Civil War there were women who fought as men. It is the same for every field, from practicing medicine to being an artist.

It is a dreadful handicap to young women who want to seek out the most challenging aspects of life when they are not aware of their history. I advise women never to let anyone tell them that they cannot do X, Y and Z because they are female.

I have been congratulated for being the first woman to compete in the Indianapolis 500, but the hard part was the thirteen years that led up to the race. I spent thousands of hours building engines alone in grubby garages because it was necessary to race and I did not have the money to pay someone to do it. Tenacity was the key to surviving the many challenges I have faced.

****

Janet Guthrie's success was short-lived. Her supporter, Kelly Girl Temporary Services, cut back their investment, and Janet's career eventually ended because she could not find financial sponsors. Her last major race was the Daytona 500 in 1980, where she finished 11th. Her groundbreaking success is reflected by the fact that her helmet and driver's suit have been displayed at the Smithsonian Institution.

Today, Janet is active in the arts and has recently finished a memoir about her experiences.

CHAPTER FOURTEEN

BILL RINALDI

It was billed as the greatest political upset in Lackawanna County in over a decade.

****

In the bicentennial year 1976, a political longshot, Jimmy Carter, became President of the United States. The movie **Rocky**, *a story about a longshot boxer who wins the heavyweight title, was a box office hit that year. As well, Bill Rinaldi left his career in teaching and took a crack at politics.*

Bill Rinaldi was born in Dunmore, Pennsylvania on July 8, 1945 and he was diagnosed with Muscular Dystrophy two years later. He is 4'11", uses a wheelchair, and is unable to do the many basic daily tasks that most people take for granted. Nevertheless, in high school, he was named as the Boy Most Likely To Succeed, Most Popular Boy, Brightest, and Mr. Personality. He also earned scholarships, medals, and other awards before graduating and going on to university.

****

At the time of my birth little was known about muscular dystrophy, so my parents did not want to "risk" having another child hence I was an only child. My mother stayed at home, while my father did menial jobs such as being a ticket agent on the graveyard shift, before becoming a deputy sheriff. They always put me first. My mother was very religious, and my father had a strong faith as well. I was cocky and self-assured due to lots of doting and positive attention from parents and relatives.

Growing up, I used my imagination to escape into worlds where I was either the third Hardy Boy or involved in some other drama. I was not a sports enthusiast, but my grandfather who was my most significant role model was, so we would watch Saturday night boxing together. My father made an effort to meet a priest who had connections to Rocky Marciano who was the heavyweight boxing champion. There was a link because we were Italians and so was Marciano. The priest arranged for us to meet Rocky and watch him train at Grossinger, New York, when I was ten years old.

Marciano established an easy rapport with me and invited me into his dressing room, and later as he went through his workouts, we talked one-on-one for a half hour. He told me how important it was to get one's mind in the right frame for focusing on whatever the goal was, whether it be training for a heavyweight fight or whatever. We visited him at least three times, and had contact by phone and mail, too. He gave me lots of signed memorabilia, which made me a hero to my friends.

While a sophomore in high school, I met John F. Kennedy at a Scranton, Pennsylvania, whistlestop. It was packed with people, and I became faint. I was taken to a side chamber where Kennedy was coming out and there I met him, and we had seven minutes of glorious conversation where he offered kind encouragement.

I took personal satisfaction in academic achievement. The high school I went to was a "jock" school where the heroes were football players. I knew that would never be an area of my personal success. I enjoyed high school yet was very apprehensive about the future and going to college. It is a scary thing when your environment changes, particularly when you have a high dependency level on others.

I attended an all-male college, the University of Scranton. My mother and father enjoyed having dorm students from there, who were far away from home, visit our house. My parents loved healthy, positive, and bright guys who accepted me. The students found a good meal and warm reception most weekends, and my dad also kept a fridge full of beer for them.

I ran for Student Body vice-president in my junior year at college. The key to the election was the debate. I did not really like a forum where I had to speak to large numbers of people, but my friend Frank said to me, "You have to win this debate." I shed my inhibitions and fears and was very confident on stage. I won the election!

A few years later, on a sunny day in 1970, I was sitting outside in our backyard wearing my bathing trunks, looking unkempt, when my grandmother, who was a wonderful, simple women, answered the phone and shoved it out the dining room window and said in a matter-of-fact tone of voice, "Some President wants to speak to you."

The phone call was so unexpected. Initially, I figured that it was one of my college buddies who was a mimic and jokester. I thought, "Here is Frank doing his Nixon thing," and that is what made it easy to talk to President Richard Nixon. It was a very light-hearted conversation at first before I began to realize the conversation was tied to a letter I had sent to the White House. The letter had discussed how, as a history teacher who loved his country, I found it tough to argue for the government position on Southeast Asia. It was obvious that I was speaking to someone who knew what was in the letter and at that point I understood who I was talking to. President Nixon talked about answering to kids who were against the Vietnam War, because he used to be a teacher, too. I brought the phone call to an end because I thought I was wasting his time because obviously he had more important things to do than to talk with me.

In 1976, I saw the movie *Rocky*, and its story of an underdog boxer helped inspire me to run for political office. I ran for Borough Tax Collector for a four-year term. I was trying to unseat the incumbent, who was a well-connected vice-president of a local bank who held a 9 to 1 advantage in voter registration. We held backyard rallies and fund-raisers, so I met many people during the campaign. It still looked like a longshot. Then on election eve, I found out that I had achieved what was billed as the greatest political upset in Lackawanna County in over a decade!

My future wife, Mary, knew me from childhood, and in the summer of 1977, when I was 32, we met again at a party and there was real romance. But the relationship didn't get started until the night of the November 1977 election, when she brought me a rose despite the fact that my political beliefs were different than her family's. On our third date I confided to her about my vulnerabilities. We married in 1989.

The last ten years have been a tough decade on my body, as aging coupled with the Muscular Dystrophy have dealt challenges. I hate seeing myself getting older and my body getting worse. In my mind I am a knight in shining armor and the armor is tarnishing over time. When I am in Florida during the winter, some think I am off in the sun having a glorious, frivolous life. We spend winters here, because my circulation leaves me freezing much of the time, and a simple cold could easily kill me.

The process of just getting ready in the course of the day is very frustrating. I have bloating and deformity of my torso, so the routine to get ready in the morning, which used to be shorter, now takes four hours. Every action is dependent, from being taken off oxygen through the process of sitting up. I now have a full-time attendant, which is comforting because it means there is another person who can help me besides my wife.

At night, after the 11 o'clock news, I receive more therapy and medication and am attached to breathing machines, which I am hooked up to throughout the night, in case my respiratory system should fail.

I pray every morning for those I see and at night for people who are gone. My family, which once numbered twenty people, all of whom I was close to, is now only two because my older relatives have died.

My life seems to go in repeated circles that just get bigger and wider, as the successes and failures seem to be relived at higher levels. God has taken me to the edge and yet it is miraculous that each time I turn around, I feel I bounce higher. After being low, I always get the strength to fight on. Find something positive in yourself and do it the best you can, and as often as you can.

****

Over 250,000 Americans have some form of Muscular Dystrophy.

Bill Rinaldi initially ran for Borough Tax Collector and later for the position of Clerk of Judicial Records for Lackawanna County, Pennsylvania. He remained undefeated in elections and held the latter position for over twenty-one years. Despite increasing health concerns, he continued to manage his staff and finish his autobiography two years ago.

Bill passed away of congestive heart failure on December 1, 2002.

CHAPTER FIFTEEN

BOB LOVE

I was alone, broke, and unable to walk without a cane. I had neither a job nor any prospect of getting one.

****

Bob Love was a professional basketball player for the Chicago Bulls in the National Basketball Association (NBA) whose biggest challenges occurred after he retired from the game.

He was born in 1942, and grew up in Louisiana. In his senior year at college, Bob made the All-South team as well as the United States national basketball team. He was selected in the fourth round of the 1965 draft by the Cincinnati Royals of the National Basketball Association.

His professional career took off when he was traded to Chicago and led the Bulls in scoring for seven consecutive years, averaging 23 points a game. The Bulls improved from being one of the worst teams in the league to being a championship contender in 1975.

****

My father, Benjamin Love, was overseas in the war. He never settled down with my mother, Lula Bell Hunter, who was only fifteen years old at the time of my birth, and he left town when I was a young child. Shortly after my birth, the plantation owner wanted my mother to go back to work. Her parents refused to let this happen, and took their whole family of twelve children plus myself and moved to a new house that only had two bedrooms.[1] Thirteen of us slept in one bedroom. We didn't have electricity until I was in high school. We relied upon kerosene lamps and had to use an outhouse.[2] We made the best of it because it was all we knew.[3]

My mother remarried, to a man who had absolutely no interest in me, because of an old rivalry he had had with my father over my mother. I never received Christmas gifts, although my stepbrothers would. My mother would later give me the toys of my brothers. One Christmas my grandparents got me a toy—a John Deere tractor. I tied a string on that little tractor and was so happy that I ran around the house about one hundred times.

I knew my mother loved me but, at age nine, after a beating from my stepfather, I left home and went back to live with my grandparents. My grandmother was a wonderful lady, and she would often give me a big hug and a kiss, which I thought was the best thing in the world. She would always carry some Juicy Fruit gum in her pocket and when I did something good she would break a little piece of the gum off and give it to me. It was very sweet and I would always try to do good things to get some. She had a strong faith, and every Sunday morning I had to get up and go to church. The only time I would come home was for dinner and then I would go back to church after eating.

We couldn't afford a basket or a ball, so I learned to play basketball by shooting rolled up socks at a wire hanger shaped like a hoop. I had a great imagination and would get lost in my dreams, pretending that I was on basketball courts with twenty or thirty thousand people in the stands, playing against the best players and always beating them.

I loved school but could not express myself because I stuttered so badly that often I could not say one word. When I was a teenager, I was the only one of my friends that did not go out on dates as I was too shy to speak. I hid my shortcomings in the world of sports and decided if I could not speak off the court, then my athletic abilities would talk for me on the court. I always dreamed and prayed that my speaking would improve.

In my senior year, the Air Force academy came by to the black high schools to try and recruit. When they came to our school in Bastrop, the whole senior class had to take their test and only three people passed: the valedictorian, another student, and Robert Earl Love, as I was known then. No one could believe that Robert Earl had passed the test. That was one of the proudest moments of my life! I wanted to go to the Air Force academy but my grandma said no, because she felt that, "Airplanes fall out of the sky."

I never realized the impact of the Civil Rights battles at the time. I was only interested in getting an education and not going back to Bastrop. In 1961, I walked five miles with 4,000 other students to the city of Baton Rouge. I will never forget that rainy, drizzly day. H. Rap Brown led us and we were singing, *We Shall Overcome*. We marched past the capital and all of a sudden the police came over a megaphone telling us to disperse. Then they started shooting the tear gas and letting the dogs loose. The dogs grabbed my coat off me and I ran all the way home.

No one thought I would go to college. I made the same grades as others in college, as there was less emphasis on expressing myself verbally and more on taking notes, passing tests or handing in papers. I was married in my senior year of college to Betty Smith, whom I had met in my junior year, and in 1965, we had our first child, Kevin.

My first year in the pros, I lived with Oscar "The Big O" Robertson (*a future Hall of Fame player who was one of the top players ever to play the game*). He took time to teach me the game and was a great help to me when I was a rookie. In 1968, I was sent to the Milwaukee Bucks, despite Oscar begging management not to trade me. The fact I stuttered so badly seemed to take away from my athletic ability in people's minds.

In Milwaukee, I scored about 18-19 points per game in preseason exhibition games, yet I was traded to Chicago. The General Manager of the Bucks at the time told me, "They had no use for me because I could not talk." I won a starting job in Chicago and never looked back.

Over my career, I had two operations on my back. In 1978, I knew it was time to retire because I could not jump or run like I used to. I figured I had a college education and with my pro background, I would have no problem getting a job.

Guys I played with, like Jerry Sloan and Bobby Weiss, got coaching jobs but I didn't. All of a sudden the reality hit me that I might not get a chance. Bobby Weiss and I golfed together, and I thought we were good friends. After retiring, when I was having a hard time, he was named the head coach for San Antonio. I asked him for a job, and he told me I was not qualified. This really hurt, and then my former coach Dick Motta did the same thing. I was the guy who had made the offense go and I knew it inside and out. I was qualified! It was always the white players who seemed to get the coaching opportunities. I was unhappy that I could not get employed anywhere that mattered to me.

After retiring, my relationship with my wife also started to go sour. We had five children by the time we divorced in 1983. One month after divorcing, I moved in with a new girlfriend, who came from the ghetto of the Chicago housing projects. We married soon after.

Shortly after the wedding I went to Los Angeles for a back operation. While I was recovering there, my new wife went back to our home in Seattle. Before long, I realized she was having an affair. It got worse, as she cashed my deferred payment checks from the Chicago Bulls. The police told me I could do nothing more than file forgery charges because she was my wife. Shortly after, she left for good and took with her most of the furniture as well. The note she left said, "I didn't want to be married to a guy who couldn't speak and I definitely didn't want to be married to a guy who's going to be a cripple for the rest of his life."[4]

It was a great shock and very devastating to me. I was alone, broke, and couldn't walk without a cane. I had neither a job nor any prospect of getting one. As well, I was behind on child support payments to my ex-wife. Life seemed so bleak. I was at my lowest point. When nighttime would come around I would get on my knees and pray. The Lord gave me the strength and courage to go on.

I did the things I had to do to get by. I used food stamps so that I could afford to feed my family even though I was divorced. I can recall hauling groceries a long distance on foot, just after I had started to walk without the use of a cane. All I could do was take two or three bags fifty yards to a place, and then go back and get the other bags. It was a one-man relay race that probably looked foolish as hell. I had to do so because there were no buses or taxis that were near my ex-wife Betty's house and I could not afford to get my old broken down car repaired.[5]

I was hired by a department store, Nordstrom, to wash dishes and bus tables for $4.45 per hour. It was a huge blow to my pride to have to do this work and it was especially difficult being seen at the store by others, including NBA players.[6] For a while, I even drove a bus at night while working there in the day. Each day, I would tell myself that it was going to get better and that no one can hold me down.

About one year after I had been working at Nordstrom, I was approached by one of the owners, John Nordstrom, and he offered to help me get my life back together by taking speech lessons.[7] In May 1986, I was sent to speech therapy, funded by Nordstrom. I was excited and enthusiastic and, one year later, I made my first public speech to 300 students. The speech went well. It was very emotional for me to talk about the toughest parts of my life — often I would get tears in my eyes. I continued public speaking and eventually became a corporate spokesman for Nordstrom. After over 43 years, my dream was coming true!

All I ever wanted was the opportunity and then I would do the best I could with it. I did not go around trying to blame this person or that person. I never wanted anyone to give me anything. I believe we have to take responsibility for anything that happens to us and have always abided by my grandmother's advice: "You got to do it yourself."

Nothing could change my dream that one day I would be able to speak without stuttering. I overcame my obstacles and now I do something that very few people can do, which is to stand in front of hundreds or thousands of people and speak. I am not perfect, but I feel I have been a good person and I have tried to help others out. I did not give up despite losing everything and having no one around me.

I have a story to tell and I am so proud because I am making a difference in the lives of young kids who say to me that they have no hope because they must live day to day. I advise them they need to start dreaming, get an education, and never give up.

You can have all the money in the world yet it can be taken away, but no one can take your faith away. Put your trust in the Lord and be a decent person. Now, every day I feel good. Sometimes when I go down the street, I have to pull over and thank the Lord for keeping me straight and strong on this long narrow road. It has been a tough journey but I have hung in there.

****

Bob's number was retired on January 14, 1994, and it is one of only three Chicago Bulls numbers to be honored that way. The other two belong to Michael Jordan and Jerry Sloan. Bob is now the Director of Community Affairs for the Chicago Bulls, and each year tells his story of perseverance to thousands of people.

CHAPTER SIXTEEN

LuAn MITCHELL-HALTER

We were told that we would never have children, and that Fred would likely not live for more than five years.

****

In 1986, just before their marriage, LuAn and Fred Mitchell received the news that Fred had cystic fibrosis, a genetic disease that affects the lungs and has a median survival age of only 33.4 years.

A short time later, a bitter feud developed within Fred's family over the direction of their sixty-year-old business, Intercontinental Packers.

****

I was twenty-two years old when I became Miss Saskatoon. In fact, the second plane ride in my life was to Toronto to compete in the Miss Canada pageant. They asked me what I was going to do for the talent part of the competition. I thought to myself, "What do I do? I don't sing or dance and I am not an actress." I decided that I should speak on the advancement of women in society and spent countless hours in the University of Saskatchewan library researching ladies who went against the odds. I think I totally bored the judges and I did not win, but it felt so right.

I was born in Melfort, Saskatchewan on December 22, 1960, the youngest of five children. My father was a brilliant high school teacher, a mathematician, and by all counts an exceptional man. He bought the Encyclopedia Britannia and Childcraft educational programs and spent many hours with us encouraging reading and learning. My mother was a homemaker and a great cook. She ended up going into the restaurant business when I was in Junior High.

In high school, I was nicknamed "Elly Mae" (*after a character in the television show The Beverly Hillbillies*) because I liked to wear button down plaid shirts and overalls, and I didn't wear any makeup. I was a cheerleader and a competitive gymnast. I was always happy and comfortable to be who I was.

After graduating, I opened a salon-spa and modeling agency. I also hosted a talk show for the cable network and FM radio station called Visual Difference. My future husband, Fred Mitchell, saw the television show, and gave me a call to see if I would go for lunch. It went well and we became very good friends. Within a year we had moved in together.

Soon after, I started to notice if I woke up in the middle of the night that Fred would not be in bed. He said that his allergies made him congested and that it helped to go outside for fresh air. But his condition seemed to me a little more than allergies. He ended up going to the Mayo Clinic in Rochester, Minnesota, and was diagnosed with cystic fibrosis.

Just before we were married, we were told that we would never have children, and that Fred would likely not live for more than five years. After we had a good cry, Fred said, "That is their prediction. I am 39, so obviously I have beaten the odds once by living this long with cystic fibrosis. I will beat the odds again." He was an optimist and whenever confronted with a challenge, he would often say, "What problem? Something better is coming down the pipe — this means we are supposed to change directions."

We were married in 1986. Lo and behold, I became pregnant, and in April of 1988, we had a beautiful baby boy. Fred became increasingly ill and his lungs got so congested that he could barely breathe. At that point he could not even pick up our child. One night he started to hemorrhage and was gushing blood while in bed. The hospital staff said he was finished. But somehow, Fred recovered enough to fly to Stanford where our only hope lay in an operation for a double lung and heart transplant.

Despite being 5'11", his weight was only about 114 pounds when he went in for the eight-hour operation. His heart, which was good and was overcompensating for two burnt-out lungs, was removed and transplanted into a 51-year-old woman. He received the heart and both lungs from a victim of a cycling accident because at Stanford they liked to transplant the lungs and heart together. The surgery went well, and miraculously he was on an exercise bike within three days and home after a few weeks. There were few complications and now the only worry was how long the transplant would work.

To get through the stress of the time, I escaped into a fictitious world and wrote. I did not care if it was good or bad writing, because it was not something I wanted to get published. The writing was just something to help me cope with the trauma of the situation. I also put together a game called Save the Planet and took it to the hospital and showed Fred. Instead of talking about his illness, we started to play this silly game. We felt that the world needed a new heart and lungs as represented by the oceans and the forests.

During that period, I also relied on my faith heavily. I became a huge believer in miracles after seeing some of the things done for Fred. For the first time in his life he could now take some deep breaths.

Before our first child in 1988, our name had been in for adoption based on the original assumption that we could not have children. Many people thought we were quite nuts when in April, 1991, we adopted a baby boy. Five months later, I found out I was pregnant, and we had our third child, a baby girl.

We were embroiled for two years in a major corporate lawsuit. Between 1994 and 1996, we suffered financially because we had put our entire life savings into the lawsuit. Some of that time we lived in a van, with three small kids and three pets, looking for consulting work for Fred. Finally, in 1996, the courts gave Fred a narrow window of opportunity to buy the company. We then had to work like heck and try to revive a virtually bankrupt enterprise.

In 1998, Fred had a follow-up visit at Stanford Hospital. While pacing in the waiting room I was told that Fred had possibly developed an allergy to one of the drugs used before a test. They told me the negative effects could not be reversed and that I was going to lose him. I fell to my knees and then flat on my face. I felt like Jell-O and was physically sick. A pastor appeared and began reading passages from the Bible. Despite the fact I was not a big person, I slammed my fist right through a wall and did not feel a thing. This was just supposed to be a checkup! The reaction continued to rapidly shut down his organs. When I heard the shrill sound of the heart monitor signifying he was gone, I kissed his cheek and made a promise to myself that I would not give up on our dream for the business.

The first and most painful thing I had to do was tell my children that their daddy had gone on to a new life. A few nights later, my oldest son, who was ten at the time, tapped me on the shoulder and asked if we would be able to pay the mortgage because he did not want to move back into the van. Fred had a beautiful butterfly collection and had spent many hours teaching the children about them. Now whenever we see one, the kids say, "There is daddy's angel."

I did not have time to mourn. I knew he would have wanted me to stay strong. On the morning of Fred's funeral, a certain individual called a board meeting. I said, "You have no right to do this. It is an insult to Fred's memory and downright cruel." I told them, "I will attend but you should know how much you are disturbing my children and the spirit of Fred Mitchell."

Some heartless people at the funeral came up to me and said, "You cannot think you are going to run the place — Fred would have wanted you to sell so that you and the kids would be looked after." Many may even have meant well with this advice, but they were wrong and very out of line. Even at the wake afterwards, individuals were telling me what I should do with the company. There were over two thousand people at his funeral.

Six months after Fred died, my wonderful mother passed away unexpectedly. All of a sudden her special and loving presence was gone. She had also been helping out with the children. Somehow, I juggled my responsibilities as a mom with my business demands thanks to the help of some friends who had kids. At the same time, the business had a big competitor opening up suddenly in Manitoba, had a new executive team installed, and was facing many other challenges. I don't think I slept for a year.

I have a problem with people who talk about glass ceilings for women as an excuse for not achieving. One of the most important things I do is avoid blaming my gender for hurdles that are present. The mindset of a disadvantaged person is very bad. I never became fearful when people said, "You cannot do that." In my opinion, being female is an advantage in business because we can bring a different perspective. I know there are opportunities out there and it is up to each individual to find them. Look in the mirror and ask yourself what you can do better and never wallow in self-pity.

I believe that the best thing you can do when facing adversity is to take an aerial view of the situation. You need to see all the landscape around, otherwise you can get caught up and swallowed by the narrow boxes of your world.

In a difficult moment, I close my eyes and try to think of the absolute worse thing that could happen and try to feel all the pain. When I am finished with that, I do not fear it as I did before. I believe experience, even if it is imaginary, is always the best teacher.

Find something that makes you feel passionate, let it envelop you and embrace it, believe with all your heart in your gut feel, and have a positive purpose for everything you are doing.

****

LuAn Mitchell-Halter refused to sell Mitchell's Gourmet Foods after her husband's death. Despite never having held a corporate job in the company, she assumed the role of chairperson. She has led the Saskatchewan-based company through five years of unprecedented expansion. Annual sales now exceed $300 million, and the company has over 1600 employees.

LuAn has earned the respect of her peers and won numerous business awards, including being named Canada's Top Female Business Owner by Chatelaine and Profit magazines for three consecutive years. She was also named to the list of Leading Women Entrepreneurs of the World, is a member of Harvard University's John F. Kennedy School of Government Women's Leadership Board, and is named as one of the 50 most influential people in the province of Alberta by Alberta Venture magazine.

CHAPTER SEVENTEEN

WILLIAM GREGORY

I was sentenced to 70 years with the possibility of parole after serving twelve years.

****

In 1993, a jury found William Gregory guilty of raping one woman, attempting to rape another woman, and committing two counts of burglary.

****

I was born December 18, 1947 and grew up in Kyle, a very small mining town in West Virginia. I was the oldest of twelve children. My grandfather had worked in the mines, and my father in a department store. We were dirt poor for a number of years. Our home had a tin roof, where bird droppings, raindrops, and even snow could be heard on it. Food was scarce, and we had to use outhouses. I can still remember my father, like in *The Grapes of Wrath*, raising his fist and vowing we would be poor no more. He joined the mines after that, and our situation improved.

My dad pushed me to do well. I was a straight A student, first-string in basketball, had a very positive attitude and good self-esteem. We went to church every Sunday, and I got along well with my parents. In fact, my dad was one of my first idols. After graduating from high school, I worked in the coal mines for a bit and then I went into the army. Shortly after that, Martin Luther King was assassinated. It depressed me and made me very afraid because I thought any black person who tried to change how society looked at blacks would be assassinated.

I ended up moving to Fort Knox, Kentucky and doing maintenance and being a jack of all trades at a nursing home until I found a career in retail management. I changed jobs a couple of times and worked at Circuit City and Sears until 1992, which is the year when the rapes occurred.

The day before I was arrested, the police had interviewed me and told me that a few people were saying I was involved with something in a parking lot. They did not even tell me the something was rape. They came to my place of work the next day and said, "We have a warrant for your arrest for rape." My first reaction was, "You gotta be kidding me; get out of here," and "Where is the camera?" "Is this candid camera?" I really said this! Then I got mad when they took me to the car. I asked them again if they were joking and they said, "We are dead serious."

On the drive to the police station, I remember them saying to me, "Come on you did it—you know you did it" and "Admit it, you raped her." I was rambling on, and in fact they used some of my statements against me in court.

One of my accusers picked me from a one-on-one police lineup, and the other recognized me because I lived in the same apartment complex. After the attempted first rape, I was kept in jail until I received bail. The second rape happened when I was out on bail. The fact I lived in the same buildings as the victims pretty well nailed the case shut, when coupled with them picking me from a police lineup. Forensic evidence appeared to indicate that hairs found were mine. This sealed my fate.

I was told to confess and I would only get six months, otherwise I might get up to 70 years. I said, "I am NOT guilty — let's go to trial." You see I was six feet tall and not 5'6" as the rapist had been described. Initially the victims could not even pick me out of photos. Physically there were major differences between myself and the suspect. The only similarity was that we were both black.

The toughest part was living in jail awaiting trial. All that was in the cell, was a commode in the middle of the room that stunk. I was thinking every phone call was the one that would free me. I kept wishing calls would come. The shock of being accused is like being a deer in the headlights. I kept thinking that this cannot be happening and I was numb all over. At first I was positive, then I lost hope and I felt like beating my head against a brick wall. I had no drive and was depressed. It is like the movie *Groundhog Day* where every day keeps repeating itself.

My fiancee went to a top lawyer in town, and he said if she had twenty thousand dollars, he was sure we could win this case. We had no money to do this. They ended up with a jury of four blacks and eight whites. It took a while to select them as they had to dismiss some potential jurors for I was well known and had a good reputation in the community.

I took to the stand and testified for myself. I was very, very nervous and swallowing and probably to the outside, looking guilty. I had asked for a lie detector test but my lawyer had ignored the request. He did not even follow-up on ideas I gave him. I felt that I was stereotyped because I was black and came from the poor section of town, and that nothing I said mattered.

The police said I was mentioning something about a VCR and a CD, which were things that only the perpetrator could have known. It frustrated me because I only knew those facts because they had told me. It was my word against theirs. I would now advise anyone to shut up and say, "Talk to my lawyer."

The jury found me guilty. The judge said to them that they could charge me for five to seventy years, and to either give the least or make an example of me. They chose to make an example of me and I was sentenced to seventy years. I felt like a fall guy. I was angry at the judge too. I was not guilty of crimes, yet I was to serve seventy years. I was not bitter at my accusers because they were likely still in shock when they picked me from the lineup.

In October 1993, I was sentenced. Entering the prison was so degrading. First they deloused me and took off my clothes, and then they threw powdery stuff all over me. I was covered from my head to the bottom of my feet and then they hosed me down. I was helpless and buck naked. I just cried right there.

The first night I was told that I had a nightmare and let out the bloodcurdling scream of a man scared to death. Some inmates said they had never heard a scream like that in their lives. Jail smells like White Castle burgers that have sat around the apartment for a day. You smell that same smell every day. Many times in jail I was threatened with death and I lived in total fear. I hung around Christian friends, and luckily the tough guys sympathized with my plight of being innocent.

My fiancee was in shock and left me. It is tough on a spouse because they feel they are locked up too, for their life is tied up and on hold. It takes an exceptional person to be able to deal with something like that. Probably the toughest moment was when my mother died while I was in prison. The captain called me in to tell me, and I cried continually for hours. I read the Bible every day all day long. I would get to a point where my faith would weaken but then I would come back strong. I took it one day at a time.

The civil trial was in 1995, and went on for fourteen days, in Louisville. It went over the same exact evidence but this time they looked at my eye color, height, and beard more closely. You could see the jury wincing and some were grabbing their mouths because my description did not match the suspect's. The forensic evidence relating to the hair samples being mine was disregarded. My lawyer, Catherine Rio, was excellent. She listened to what I had to say, asked good questions, and got the right responses.

I felt so good when I was found innocent. I thought the world would listen to me and my case would be reopened after the civil trial verdict but it did not mean anything. The good feeling only lasted a week. After the trial I went back to the prison. Nobody had listened or noticed the trial. Even my pastor was telling me it would take me fifteen years to get out of prison as he thought I was guilty. He even said to me, "Maybe, William, you forgot you did it."

George Edwards, who was a volunteer at area prisons, heard of my plight through another prisoner who was convinced I was innocent. George and his wife took up my cause. They got Barry Sheck's foundation, The Innocence Project, to help. Mr. Sheck came to me and said he could get me out in two months but that I had to wait as he had two people on death row to free first. Waiting was very tough and a true test of my faith. Any inmate will tell you they do not believe anything until they see it. With the advance of DNA testing, I was found to be not guilty.

I was freed on July 5, 2000. I had been in prison for over six years. When I came out, the cameras were on me and I spoke to the media and said, "I need help—I am sick because of what happened to me."

There were many changes I noticed after coming out of prison. Using a debit card, working a gas pump with a charge card, and grocery checkouts all proved challenging. The Internet was all new to me—click on this, pull on this, type something in—it did not make sense at first. I was frustrated, and felt the job market had passed me by. I am still having problems adjusting to computers.

I am currently working at Walgreens Drug Store earning $7 per hour, but am hoping to get into a manager position and earn in the range of $13-14 per hour. It is frustrating to feel that I am behind because of the time I lost. I am angry that I have had no apology, just some official document saying I will not be bothered by the police.

The only way I got through this ordeal was with my faith and the help of people who believed in my innocence. I couldn't go through it on my own. I realize the pain will not go away, deep problems are still in there and I try to face up to my worries and fears.

No matter what your situation, do not give up even though sometimes it seems easy to do so. My faith gave me hope.

Trust in God completely.

****

William is free today because George Edwards, a retired Presbyterian theologian, and his wife went on a five-year mission to raise more than $5,000 in order to get DNA testing. With help from the Innocence Project founded by Barry Sheck and Peter Neufeld, William was found to be not guilty after he had spent over 50,000 hours in prison.

Since the advent of DNA testing in the late 1980s, according to the Innocence Project, at least sixty-three people in the United States have been exonerated specifically through DNA testing of their evidence. Overall, the Innocence Project has helped reverse or overturn over 100 cases.

According to Dr. Bruce Hardy, (William's psychologist), he is still showing classic signs of post-traumatic stress syndrome as evidenced by flashbacks and depression. William is currently trying to raise money for the Kentucky Innocence Fund which two years ago had only $10,000 and many cases to deal with.

CHAPTER EIGHTEEN

JIM MCKENNY

I was an unemployed 32-year-old with a tenth grade education and I owed $90,000 to Revenue Canada.

****

Jim McKenny's toughest challenges in life came after his professional hockey playing days ended.

In the mid 1960s, Jim McKenny dominated Junior Hockey. He was compared to Bobby Orr, who was the best defenceman at that time, and who was held by general consensus to be the best ever to play the game.

Jim was drafted by the Toronto Maple Leafs in 1963. They were a powerhouse in the 1960s and won Stanley Cups in 1962-64 and 1967. It was a very tough team for a young player to crack because it was full of all-stars and veterans. Despite being a highly touted prospect, he spent his first professional years playing in the minors. He finally made the team and started to play regularly in the late 60s.

He built a name for himself as a solid hockey player; not as another Bobby Orr, but as Jim McKenny. His professional career spanned 604 games, and 329 total points. It ended when he was 31. He also created an equally large reputation for himself off the ice as a man who loved to have fun.

****

My father, Claude, was a military officer who became a veteran of three wars. I lived on several military bases while growing up, due to my father's frequent transfers. This helped me to form a fighting spirit at an early age, because each new home always led to someone challenging me, as the new kid, to a fight. I was a good athlete, headstrong, and had a sense of humor, but I was painfully shy.

I was selected in the third round, #17 overall in 1963. At that time you were owned by the NHL team that sponsored the Junior team you played for. This meant I would be part of the Toronto Maple Leafs system. I was sent to the minors after my first training camp with the team. Being sent down and then realizing I was only a fringe player on a minor league team was a kick in the teeth. It was a very low and depressing point in my life. All my self-doubts and fears, that were not apparent to outsiders, reappeared.

While in the minors in Rochester, my roommate was Don Cherry (*now one of Canada's highest profile media personalities*), and he, as well as my teammates, saved me by not allowing me to completely lose confidence in my abilities. The minors allowed me to work hard at my game in a less pressure-filled environment, and within three years I had learned and improved enough to be brought up to the Maple Leafs full-time for the start of the 1968-69 season.

The NHL was utopia for me. I was being paid to play hockey and had the camaraderie of my teammates as well as the freedom to party every night. In professional hockey, everything is done for you. My only responsibility was to be on time for the buses. It was a great life that was only interrupted by two to three hours when we had to play a game. I was told by the Maple Leafs to curtail my drinking or I would be gone. As a result, I switched to marijuana and continued my lifestyle.

The sixties and seventies were a period when owners controlled the players. You were told what to sign for and there was no negotiating. I think my first contract was for $6,000 per year. My pay rose dramatically when I signed a five-year contract for $120,000 in 1972. In my mind that meant I would never have to work another day after hockey. I paid absolutely no attention to finances, because I felt that was the agent's job.

During the 1976 Canada Cup tournament my teammate on the Toronto Maple Leafs, Borje Salming, who was playing for Sweden at the time, received a standing ovation from the Canadian crowd. I was very close to Borje; as one of the first Europeans to play in the NHL, he had endured a lot of abuse. It was one of the most emotional moments of my life and it remains my favorite hockey memory.

My professional career ended at age 31 when I was sent to the minors in Dallas. I thanked my coach at the time, Roger Neilson, for sending me there. The minors were less pressure and an incredible amount of fun as I got to play on a regular basis and meet some great people that I still consider friends after twenty years. I made second team all-star in Dallas but was traded for nothing to Minnesota, and then finished up in Oklahoma City. I was unready to give up the game, so I went to Switzerland and later France to play hockey. I was paid a pittance compared to what I had been earning in the NHL. The writing was on the wall, and I knew my career was over. The final straw came when my wife, whose interior design career was starting to take off, told me to come home or she would leave me. I resented the ultimatum, but I returned to Canada anyway and retired from hockey.

I have omitted mentioning my wife to this point, because I was an absentee father and husband. I had gotten married in 1965 at age nineteen to my best friend's sister who was seventeen at the time. By the time I returned from Europe, my daughter was fourteen and my son eleven, and I did not know either of them very well. It is a miracle that my wife stayed with me through the first fifteen years of our marriage.

My first stop back in Canada was to visit my agents and see if they could help find me work. I was shocked when they handed me all my files and told me that I was of no value to them as a retired player. It was a harsh reality as I realized I was on my own. The second hit came when Revenue Canada informed me that I owed them $90,000. A tax shelter that had been devised by my agents was ruled illegal by their tax people. I had never looked at my finances before this point, and all my money that had not been spent was tied up in long-term annuities, which I could not access.

Being famous enough to be recognized on the streets was of little comfort. I was unemployed, with only a tenth grade education and no marketable skill. My first year working, I think I earned about $1,200 doing small bits of modeling and acting. When my wife saw my tax slip which showed how little income I had earned for the year, she went through the roof. I knew I had to find some real employment.

My first two jobs were selling for different divisions of Avenue Television and Telecommunications. Both were disasters that drove my confidence down even further. I never quit either job because that wasn't me, but I was very relieved both times when I was told that I was being let go. It was just as well, because I can't remember making any sales. I was incredibly depressed, and absolutely seething with anger at the world.

The only release during those bleak days was running ten miles every day alone with my dog. It was the only escape I had. I started working at a radio station and doing some air time for free. Over the next sixteen years, I worked and improved and became the anchor for the sports broadcasts for CityTV in Toronto. I was driven by the fear of falling back to the state I had been in during the first few years after retirement.

I finally have stability in my life, which is quite a change considering I have moved at least 48 times. I am now recognized for my television career and not for hockey. Recently I embraced spirituality, and I credit it with finally bringing peace and happiness to my personal life. That, combined with a stable career, have made the last twelve years the best of my life.

Whatever comes my way, I will deal with and accept, because I know that God is applying the direction and knowing this has taken away my fears of the future. I have learned from my ups and downs that we take life for granted. It is precious and we spend too much time worrying. I now live to enjoy each day thoroughly and am no longer in a fragile state.

In the past, when difficult moments arose, I would blame others and escape to another night or week of partying. My turnaround occurred when I took responsibility for my future and ceased blaming others. I stopped escaping the challenges I was enduring which allowed me to set the foundation for a new career. I did not quit trying despite years of frustration and self-imposed humiliation.

If you are having problems, give up your life to God and ask for his guidance. Do whatever is put in front of you. The outcome is God's will. No one is dying of terminal uniqueness, in that we are all basically the same. God has worked for millions of others and will work for you.

The bad days that I have now are my glory days, and I learn from them and don't fear them at all.

****

Jim McKenny is now best known as the sports anchor for a television station (CityTV) in Toronto where his trademark sense of humor and strong personality are evident.

He is one of the city's most recognizable faces—again.

CHAPTER NINETEEN

SARAH BRADY

There were many tense moments during the five-hour surgery and the days following.

****

Sarah Brady's husband, Jim, was the White House press secretary for President Ronald Reagan's administration. On March 30, 1981, John W. Hinckley Jr. attempted to assassinate President Reagan, and a stray bullet hit Jim Brady, leaving him with permanent brain damage.

Four years later, Sarah Brady became a spokesperson for improved gun control and, in 1989, she was named the Chair of Handgun Control Incorporated. Despite strong opposition from groups such as the NRA, she persevered and, on November 30, 1993, watched President Clinton sign into law the "Brady Bill," named for her husband. The bill required a five-day waiting period and background check on all handgun purchases through licensed dealers.

****

Prior to Jim joining the Reagan administration, we lived like normal average people who entertained casually at home and rarely traveled. I preferred being at small gatherings with close friends. The changes that occurred in our life after he became Press Secretary were unreal. For us it was like living in a dream world and I don't think either of us could quite believe it.

Before going to Washington, if we went to a big party everyone put their coats on a bed in the back bedroom. All of a sudden we were attending large parties at places like Katherine Graham's house with valet parking and a coat check room, meeting elegant folks and people I had only read about. Everyone was very gracious, and yet it was fairly intimidating for me at the beginning.

Everything changed March 30, when Jim was wounded in the shooting. We felt lucky because he had made it through the five-hour surgery and the days following. Seeing other patients on the neurosurgery floor who were far worse off reinforced how fortunate we were. I started to look around at all the other families and I saw people without insurance, or with insurance that did not cover all their costs. Some patients had been in car accidents, a few had brain tumors, and others had a variety of terrible things. It was a ward full of very serious cases. If a person staying there was going to make it at all, their life was going to be drastically changed.

We had so much support from family and friends. I always felt that the publicity surrounding Jim and the assistance we received from people we did not even know was a source of inspiration for us. Jim still uses the line, "I guess if you are going to go out and get shot it doesn't hurt to be with the President of the United States."

Instead of complaining, I tried to make our new life as good as possible. I avoided self-pity. We all have moments when we feel sorry for ourselves, but throughout my life I have always felt that it was such a weakness to do so. In the background of our challenges, my faith was also there, and I know that it helped me.

It was most evident in those first years after the shooting how much our life had changed. My initial instinct was that I wanted things to get back to normal. We tried to recreate wonderful times from the past by renting a beach house for a weekend that we associated with fun vacation memories. But that turned out to be a very tough weekend because it showed us that Jim was not as energetic or enthusiastic as he had been before. It told us that we could not go back and relive the life we had before the shooting. This message was given to us quite a few times. We needed to adjust to what we currently had and go from there.

On a summer day in 1985, we were visiting my husband's hometown of Centralia, Illinois. A friend owned a construction company and one of her workers came by in his truck to pick us up and take us swimming at her place. Our son Scott, who was six, jumped in first, and then I got in. Scott grabbed what I thought was a play gun and started looking at it and treating it casually, waving it around. I took it and told him to never point a toy gun at anyone. It was then that I realized that it was not a toy, but a little .22 handgun. I started shaking and could not believe that it had just been lying there. My mind kept dwelling on it.

We had just gotten back from that trip when I happened to be listening to the evening news and heard that the NRA was pushing an upcoming bill in the Senate that would have obliterated the 1968 gun control law that set age limits for gun buyers, among other things. I had already thought that common sense gun laws were important, but I had chosen not to get involved until that point. Hearing about this proposed legislation just after what had happened with Scott was certainly the icing on the cake. I called the NRA and told them they would have to reckon with me—as if they cared at that point. I then called Handgun Control and I got involved working for improved gun control.

We cared for the issue very deeply. What we were fighting for was such common sense. I thought it would be a quick battle and then we would get back to a normal life. After a year or two it became evident how difficult it would be to change things. My staff shielded me from a lot of the ugly personal letters and calls. There was a polarization that occurred because each side tried to paint the other side as extremists. They wanted to portray us as gun grabbers. It was part of the game. Jim and I had been in politics all of our lives and understood that. The political battle was one of the few parts of our prior life that we could incorporate into our new life. Today, it still bothers me to hear misinformation about the cause, but it comes with the territory.

The biggest day for us, singularly, was when the Brady Bill first passed the House of Representatives. To know we had won was out of this world! Finally having President Clinton, who worked hard for it as well, sign it into law a couple of years later was also a wonderful day.

By 2000, I had reduced my workload with Handgun Control and we were enjoying a more relaxing pace of life. Then, in March of that year, I found out that I had lung cancer. I was told that it had spread to the lymph nodes in my chest.

The first days after I found out were the hardest because I was thinking I would die immediately. Then I got busy with the work of ascertaining my treatment plan and who I should see. This got my mind off the eventuality of what could happen. Amazingly enough, once I started therapy, I learned to enjoy each day and savor life. Things got easier as I learned to adjust and not try to do too many things at once.

Today, everything for Jim and me is more family-oriented. Money issues and our 401K reserves are not going to bother us, because we have our lives. It is not always easy to do, but we try to stay focused on what's important in life and not stress over insignificant things. Life's little hassles seem insignificant now.

Until you have a tragedy, you are always waiting for something: your future driver's license, getting married, waiting to have your children, then waiting to retire. We spend our lives planning for the future instead of living for today. One thing survivors have learned to do is enjoy the moment. We do not know what the future holds and there is nothing we can do about it anyway.

Live for today.

****

Since March 2000, Sarah Brady has undergone chemotherapy, radiation, and other treatments to battle the cancer. She is doing well, although her overall prognosis is uncertain. She also became a published author and traveled the country promoting her book, titled **A Good Fight.**

CHAPTER TWENTY

MIKE UTLEY

Man, I wish I could take that one play back!

****

Mike Utley's high school football coach Tom Merrill stated, "Mike Utley was the greatest football player in the history of John F. Kennedy High School in Seattle, Washington." He received a scholarship to Washington State University in 1984, and competed there for four years, in his last year leading them to their most successful season since 1929. Mike became only the second player in the university's history to earn consensus first team All-American honors. He joined the Detroit Lions in 1989.

****

Growing up, my idols were my parents and my two older brothers. I was the first to start and last to leave when all of us would wrestle with my dad. I loved all sports, especially football, and was always playing with the older kids. After a while, I got tired of getting beaten by the bigger kids, which forced me to improve.

My father was a mechanical engineer at Boeing and my mother was a registered nurse. Dad worked Monday to

Friday and Mom worked the 3rd shift at the hospital, so there was always one parent home. I learned my work ethic from my parents. They sacrificed and gave it all for us.

I weighed 295-310 pounds in university and had 10% body fat (*an average male under thirty years of age has 17% body fat*). I started studying business and then switched to general studies. School was tough for me, because although I knew the answers, something got messed up on the way from my brain to the pen and the result was not what I thought it was. By the end, I just wanted to get out of there.

In 1989, I was drafted in the third round by the Detroit Lions. The biggest difference between university football and the pros is how fast things happen around you. The time to absorb, process, and react is much shorter in the pros. Many times I said to myself, "What am I doing here?"

I entered training camp at 306 pounds and was doing two workouts per day for seven weeks. I ate between 8,000 to 10,000 calories per day to maintain my weight. I would have, at minimum, a dozen egg whites, two to three cans of fish and chicken, one-and-a-half pounds of flank steak, potatoes, salad, and lots more. The feeling you have after Thanksgiving dinner is what I felt six times a day. Every three hours I ate a full meal, and I was committed to doing it.

In my first year with the Lions, I found myself in the starting lineup playing right guard. The week of my first NFL start was a dream come true. I could tell myself that I was among the elite players in the world, and that I would be playing against the best of the best. I was wound very tightly before the first game, but that feeling quickly went away the first time I was smashed upside the head by the man I was blocking.

I was injured my first year, in the fifth regular season game, when my right leg snapped on a hit four inches above the knee. The sound of the break was so loud it could be heard on the sidelines. We were playing the Minnesota Vikings, and I remember one of their players saying to me, "Stay down—they do not pay us enough for this." I was embarrassed to be carried off the field, and told myself I would never be carried off again.

In my second year, my eleventh and twelfth ribs became vertical on a hit. I returned after a few games but one of my own guys hit my elbow and rotated my arm up which separated my shoulder. I was paying my dues and learning how to suck it up and play with pain. In 1991, I regained my starting position, and finally had the system down. No one was going to take my job away from me.

During a game against the Los Angeles Rams on November 17, 1991, I blocked an opponent, fell to the ground and knew immediately that something bad had happened. I had lost all feeling from my chest down. I managed to give a thumbs up as I was being taken off the field to the hospital. I did that because I wanted to make sure the fans knew that I heard them cheering for me.

I was told in the hospital that, because the sixth and seventh vertebrae in my neck were crushed, I would be paralyzed. The greatest risks with my injury were either blood clots or having fluid fill the lungs. Thanksgiving night I was back in the Intensive Care Unit and had two blood clots on my lungs, which was a very serious condition, but over time I recovered.

Initially, there were a lot of things I could not do. I lost 105 pounds very quickly, as I was not getting enough calories per day to maintain my weight. I looked at myself and thought, "Dude, you look awful."

Herb Walsh, the Defensive Back for the Lions, was a close friend and he came to see me right away. He went back and told the guys on the team that I was still the same person, but not a lot of my teammates came to visit. You must understand that the mentality of an athlete is that they do not want to see that they can get hurt like this. Out of sight, out of mind. Chuck Schmidt, the General Manager of the Lions, visited me and gave me all I needed and to this day, they still take care of me.

My parents and family were a great support. My brothers still treated me the same. In 1991, just before Christmas, one brother put Christmas lights on my halo (*a brace worn on the head to stabilize the neck and spine*) and obviously I could not do anything to get them off which he thought was pretty funny. But I got my brothers back.

One of my favorite times was when my brother Paul came to visit. I gave him a spare wheelchair, and we raced uphill to the mailbox. Of course I let him win because he was the older brother. Then I said, "OK, now let's race back." I counted one, two, three, Go! He gave two hard pushes and was off. I just stayed where I was. He was going downhill out of control and ended up having to grab the rims of the wheels and burned his hands trying to stop his chair. I was wearing gloves and cautiously went down the hill.

When I first got injured, everyone was worried that I might kill myself because there is a very high suicide rate with people who have suffered spinal cord injuries. Luckily, I am positive and I like living life to the fullest. It probably sounds hokey, but I do not remember any time when I was down. Maybe it was because of the athletic training, which teaches you to not remember the negative stuff. In football, if I screwed up on a play, I had to get over it and let it go. I never lost my zest and fight for life.

There are certain rules to being paralyzed that one must follow, but they can be bent. I have certain limitations due to my size, but I can still work out in a weight room, and I enjoy getting out on the water, either kayaking, boating, seadooing, or water-skiing. It is most important to me to be able to do personal stuff by myself. Biofeedback and hard work allowed me to once again use my hands to shave, brush my teeth, and cook.

I thank God for making me a football player. Not everyone is 6'6" and 300 plus pounds. I realize that I must give my respect back to God for all I have, by always giving 100%. Faith has always been there from day one.

I met my future wife Dani in 1998 at Gold's gym in Wenatchee, Washington. She knew nothing about football or who I was. I kept asking her out, and she never said yes, but she never said no, so there was hope. Finally after some time, I broke her down. Since July 1998, we have been together. The most afraid I have ever been was asking her mom if I could marry her daughter. We were married on Friday the thirteenth, July 2000.

The Utley Foundation was set up in 1992 to help find a cure for paralysis. Currently, we are trying to raise 1.5 million dollars for research, as well as looking for people with ideas who want to help in some way or to volunteer their time. I am hopeful, and believe a cure will come. I realize not everyone can give money, but I hope that people, regardless of the cause they choose to support, will get involved and help somebody at least one day of the week or month.

I volunteer and enjoy helping children with spinal cord injuries by challenging them to do something and seeing them get to the next level. It is very rewarding to see a kid trying to stand for the first time. My message to the kids is that you have to live. You have to do your business and be functional. Do the little things, like taking care of yourself and making sure you look good. Be a productive part of society. I challenge them to do something today that they did not do yesterday, and tomorrow to do something that they did not do today.

I get frustrated with paralyzed people who complain and sit waiting for science to cure them. I believe you must get out and live life to the fullest now. We all make choices. If you do not like the choice you made, then change it.

I wish that the play that injured me had never happened. However, I know that the only injury that could have truly changed me is one to my head. I focus on what I can do. The only thing I cannot do is play football but, at age 37, I am now too old to play anyway. I strongly believe that tough times never last but tough people do.

Every chance you get, you had better enjoy yourself, because you might not get the chance again for your heart has only so many beats. You need to forget the negative outcomes. What you need to remember is what you have to do in the future. People succeed by doing small things that are built one on top of the other. This is what gets you to the top of the mountain. You have to take the first step.

****

Through biofeedback (retraining the brain to make unconscious bodily processes detectable to the senses, so that they can be controlled consciously) and hard work, Mike has regained strength in his upper body, and is very active in weight training and other recreational activities.

Mike and his wife Dani work as a team promoting the Mike Utley Foundation, which is dedicated to finding a cure for paralysis.

CHAPTER TWENTY-ONE

PATTY WETTERLING

I was in total disbelief and shock. My son Jacob had been kidnapped.

****

On October 22, 1989, Patty and Jerry Wetterling's eleven-year-old son, Jacob, was abducted at dusk by a masked gunman who cornered him, his younger brother, and a friend on their way back from a local store. Only Jacob was taken.

The local police of St. Joseph (a small community of approximately 3,000 people northwest of Minneapolis/St. Paul, Minnesota), and the F.B.I. had no success tracking down the kidnapper despite numerous leads.

****

I was born November 2, 1949 in Omaha, Nebraska, and moved to Minnesota when I was a young girl. My father died when I was five years old, and my mother later remarried. I was very lucky, because my family provided tremendous support. My positive nature certainly came from this wonderful upbringing, and my strength was deep rooted.

I went to teacher's college at Mankato State University in Mankato, Minnesota and then went on to teach my first year in Maryland. I taught high school equivalency to merchant marines on a ship. The library was in the engine room but it was an amazing experience. I was on the ship for a year. The toughest thing was making them believe that they could learn.

When I was twenty-three years old, I returned to Minnesota and married Jerry Wetterling. He went back to school to be a chiropractor, so I taught and helped to put him through school. We started a family in 1976 when we had Amy. Next was Jacob in February, 1978, Trevor in the fall of 1979, and finally, Carmen in September, 1981.

On October 22, 1989, Jacob, Trevor, and another boy took their flashlights and went to the store after dark. On the way back, a masked gunman stopped them and asked each of them how old they were. He told Trevor and the other boy to run off into the woods and not look back. When Trevor looked back, Jacob and the man were gone. My son Jacob had been kidnapped.

When I was told, I was in total disbelief and shock. I have very little memory of the first three weeks other than being immobile and depressed. It became impossible for my husband and me to talk to each other and our relationship deteriorated. It got worse because law enforcement kept asking us questions about each other. We both became suspicious of what the other person was saying and we could deal only with matter of fact issues in our relationship.

It took us three years to return to a semblance of normalcy. Marriage is hard on a good day for anyone. We refused to put our other kids through any more trauma like a separation and, as time went by, our marriage got better. It was a huge commitment to make it work!

Trevor was terrified and spent one and a half years sleeping in our bedroom as he could not sleep at nights. We worked really hard helping him to cope with his guilt so that he would accept that there was nothing he could have done.

I aligned myself with law enforcement because I felt they had the key to finding Jacob. Jerry tried psychics hoping to find information that would help us. He spent hours talking to them and never slept.

Jerry went back to work and resumed some sense of order in his life before I did. He knew we had to get some money in and, if he went to work, that would help the kids get back to school. I was never able to go back to any of the stuff I used to do. Many times we had to drop everything we were doing and go meet the F.B.I. agents about a lead. Luckily, Jerry had friends who helped him out with his business when he was called away suddenly. I had no job to go back to because I had been a stay-at-home mom. I felt like I had flunked in the very thing I had committed my life to doing.

We had so much support, especially at the start. Our community is very family oriented and they have been wonderful to us. We were both just trying to survive this thing at first. After a while, it became a challenge to figure out how to keep media still involved and the word out so that we might find Jacob. We started the Jacob Wetterling Foundation, which I would not recommend to others in the same situation because it is grueling. It was like starting a new business where you have to manage the books and other aspects all while under tremendous stress.

I probably drove the F.B.I. and law enforcement crazy. One day, an agent asked me how I got rid of stress. I replied that I used to dance, but nothing inside me could do it anymore. He told me I needed to get on a program and exercise so I began walking, running, and swimming. This saved me as it let me clear my head and stop the agony from eating me.

Our kids have been the shining stars. They have shown us how to live again by dragging us out to do things and teaching us how to laugh again. It took months to laugh without guilt and even then it was forced. As time went by it became more normal. Amy grew up way too fast and was married in December 2001. Carmen, the youngest, initially was very confused and reverted back to her imaginary friends and thumbsucking, while Trevor attended school in Colorado. I could not have survived if it was just for me but I could for them.

The phone ringing still drives us nuts. I am always looking for something interesting or different in the mail or on our call display that might mean something. I have to believe that a phone call, knock on the door, or letter in the mail will provide an answer. We have to live with not knowing. It is like holding your breath. It is an agonizing anticipation we still carry.

I believe there is a chance that Jacob is still alive. I have envisioned us being reunited and going on a family trip to an island or Europe and getting to know each other and rebuilding our relationship. I have also thought about the possibility of him being dead. We would need proof if he were not alive, and if that were the case, then the question would be, "Who did it?" The worst scenario is that he is alive and being treated poorly. I try not to spend a lot of energy on negative thoughts.

The perpetrator needs to be caught and I will continue to try to help make this happen. I refuse to let the man who abducted Jacob take anything more away from me. He cannot take my marriage, my outlook, or my faith in God. It is a battle between him and me and I am not going to let him win.

I wrote a letter in 1999, which was published in state newspapers. It was directed at Jacob's abductor. It talked about Jacob, and also asked the kidnapper about his life. The idea for the letter to the abductor came from a woman who had done the same, and the abductor and murderer of her child called her and they talked for an hour. She was a deeply religious person who worked very hard to forgive the person who did it. I do not know if I could ever achieve that level of faith. I was willing to try anything that had been tried in the past, to see if this would be the one thing that provided some information. There was no response to the letter.

The foundation and prevention education takes up a lot of my time today, as well as a parent support group, called Team HOPE, that I have helped to start. It is a strengthening experience, and I am excited and proud of the work we have done. It is heartening and rewarding to help others who have missing children.

Our recovery started slowly, by first getting out of bed one day and then getting dressed. It took little baby steps initially. Learning to accept help was difficult. You should let go of negative people and thoughts. Hold on to what is good in your life. Try to find and believe in your dreams, and do not give up on them. I yelled at God and felt anger because I could not understand how this could happen, but I have to believe that he is with Jacob, and taking care of him. I believe in miracles and hope that if I pray enough, good will happen. The world can be better.

I do believe hope is what carried me. I look at "hope" as an action word, because you must get out there and work. I am fighting for my son, for I would do anything to preserve how Jacob saw the world. No one can take away the eleven years we had. I cannot let go of what he believed in just because someone did a terrible thing.

You must fight for how you want life to be.

****

Patty Wetterling was listed as one of the 100 most influential Minnesotans of the 20th century as selected by Minnesota's largest newspaper, the Star Tribune.

In 1994, Congress passed the Jacob Wetterling Act, which forced states to initiate sex offender registration programs. The Jacob Wetterling Foundation mandate is to protect children from sexual exploitation and abduction. It has helped to find missing children and educate children, teens, parents, caregivers, and teachers about personal safety. It is estimated that in the United States, 4,600 non-family abductions occur each year.

The Wetterlings continue to look for Jacob today.

CHAPTER TWENTY-TWO

NICK BRENDON

My biggest fear was being in front of people.

****

Nick Brendon is best known for the role of Xander Harris on the hit television series, **Buffy the Vampire Slayer.** *The show was a tremendous success and lasted seven seasons.*

Nick paid his dues doing commercials and performing in various guest roles before taking time away from acting. He struggled with a variety of other jobs ranging from delivering food to waiting on tables before returning to acting and successfully auditioning for the role of Xander Harris.

****

When I was seven or eight my stuttering became apparent. It happened shortly after a day when my twin brother Kelly went missing for two hours. After this trauma occurred, it was as if my brain got wounded and I had a hard time saying words. I do not even remember talking before I stuttered. It took over and held me back, especially when I was in junior high and high school.

I did not get a lot of speech therapy outside of school. It was a slow process, but I retrained myself to talk using tongue twisters, and step-by-step I learned how to work my tongue and lips. I also got over stuttering by calming down, asking myself why it was happening, and recognizing what the problem was. The stuttering did not stop overnight.

Stuttering held me back from dating and approaching girls, so instead I got into baseball and played rightfield during high school and college. Baseball players were my idols and because I grew up in California, I wanted to emulate pretty much all the Los Angeles Dodger players.

When I was twenty, I still stuttered, I had low self-confidence, and my parents were getting divorced. I had a talk with God and decided to confront my fears and take an acting class despite the fact that my biggest phobia at that time was being in front of people. The class was nerve-wracking but it helped me learn to concentrate better. I managed to control my speech during auditions, but still stuttered occasionally while working.

I had two separate acting careers. I acted from age twenty-one to twenty-three, took a couple of years off, and then got back into it with *Buffy the Vampire Slayer*. The first time I was very worried about my speech and afraid I would stutter. I was not having fun. I quit acting and worked a variety of jobs to pay the bills. It sucked. Enough is enough, is how I felt after all the jobs. Because of the wide variety of jobs that I have done, I feel that I am well covered for any character I will have to play.

When I got back into acting my whole perspective had changed because I felt that it was my time to succeed. I loved the fact that acting was a constant challenge that allowed me to be artistic and express myself. I was having fun and just trying to make a good impression as opposed to feeling I had to get the job. This attitude helped, because I tended to stutter when I felt pressure.

Once we saw the first three episodes of the show *(Buffy the Vampire Slayer)*, I knew we were doing something really good. We were fortunate because Warner Brothers television channel was just starting out and they had no one-hour shows. We felt that this meant that our show would be on for a while if the quality was passable, and we were lucky because it turned out to be a great series.

There is no class that prepares you for when you find your anonymity is gone, so you kind of take it one challenge at a time. If people want your autograph it means you are doing a good job and you should sign for them because it is in the unwritten contract. Being recognized opens doors but you have to know what you can and cannot say and where you can and cannot go.

When I am having a difficult time, I talk to God, meditate, and listen to music. The pain that accompanies any letdown in life tends to numb after a while. At the lowest points when my mood is being affected, I tell myself, "This is not how you truly view life." I rely on both myself and my family, depending on what the situation is. Faith also helps me keep things in perspective.

Overcoming stuttering has given me confidence even though it was painful when I would lapse. It has been an honor to be a spokesman for the Stuttering Foundation of America and being asked to do it two years in a row made me feel that I have been able to help. Succeeding at acting is also something I am very proud of doing.

When you are facing adversity, you should analyze why you are where you are. Realize that life is precious. Ask yourself, "Are you really happy and do you know what makes you happy?"

As long as you feel something, whether it's joy or sadness, you can be inspired to get up off the floor and try again.

****

What makes Nick Brendon's acting career remarkable is that he is one of three million Americans who stutter. Roughly one percent of the population has this communication disorder, although it affects males at a much greater rate than females. Winston Churchill, Marilyn Monroe, Bruce Willis, and singer Carly Simon all have had to battle stuttering. There are no clear-cut answers as to the causes, and according to the Stuttering Foundation of America (SFA), it may occur when a variety of factors merge. There is no quick fix, but speech therapy can make a significant difference.

Through hard work, training, and speech therapy, Nick has overcome stuttering and helped others by going public with his story.

CHAPTER TWENTY-THREE

W MITCHELL

"He seems so positive and upbeat, but what is he going to do when he realizes how terrible it is?"

****

On a beautiful San Francisco summer morning on July 19, 1971, Mitchell flew solo in an airplane for the first time. Later that same day, he took a ride on his new motorcycle, and the perfection of his day shattered.

A laundry truck made an illegal turn, and Mitchell crashed into its side. The gas cap came off the motorcycle, and fuel leaked onto the engine creating a fiery explosion. Mitchell suffered burns to over 65% of his body and was in a coma for two weeks. The accident badly burned his face and left him without fingers. His recovery was slow and painful.

Over the next two years, Mitchell invested in real estate and in a project manufacturing a new type of fuel-efficient stove. The investments proved successful and made him a millionaire. He even bought a Cessna and resumed flying again.

****

I was born April 11, 1943, just outside of Philadelphia. I was the youngest of three with two wonderful sisters. My dad was in the insurance business in an administrative capacity. He was a wonderful part of my life, and we spoke on the phone every day for the last ten years of his life. He lived to be 97.

My mom and dad divorced when I was five. She remarried when I was six, and my stepdad, Luke Mitchell, was my idol. I adored him because he was an all-around great guy. He was a gentleman, charming, gracious, an equestrian, and had been an officer in the cavalry of World War One. He died of cancer when I was 17 years old. I was very lucky to have had two great role models in my father and stepfather.

In 1960, after leaving school, I decided to join the marines, where I soon learned I had fewer answers than I thought. I got out just before Vietnam and after passing my entrance exam, enrolled at the University of Hawaii. I was really not much of a student, as I was too easily distracted. I left Hawaii before I graduated and went back to Philadelphia.

I was not focused on being excellent at anything. I tried a number of different jobs, ranging from disc jockey, bartender, encyclopedia salesman, substitute schoolteacher, taxi driver, to going into insurance. I loved the variety and did whatever I wanted.

As a tribute to my stepfather, I had my name legally changed to W. Mitchell with a period after the W. Later, I decided I wanted to be referred to as Mitchell so I took out the period after the W, and my name became W Mitchell. My friends just call me Mitchell.

I moved out west to San Francisco and found employment working as a gripman operating a cable car. I was one of only sixty people in the world that did this job. As a gripman, you can be a ham and feel as if you are onstage, while doing something truly unique. It was a fascinating adventure. San Francisco is one of the most beautiful places to work. It was an all-around great opportunity that allowed me to meet wonderful people, tourists, and pretty girls while getting paid well. The guys who worked on the cable cars were an eclectic group of writers and thinkers. It was a real bohemian experience.

Looking back on the motorcycle accident, I do not have a solid recollection of what was going through my mind afterwards. I didn't spend a lot of time thinking that it was the end of the world. I was frustrated, angry, and had all types of emotions. I certainly recall being depressed, and I may have blotted out some of the bad stuff, but I didn't have long spells of despair.

I remember my mother visiting me one or two months after the accident, and saying to others, "He seems so positive and upbeat, but what is he going to do when he realizes how terrible it is?" There are some people who dwell each day on how awful things are, and they live in a delusional world where everything is perceived to be so bad. I do not think I ever realized how "terrible it is."

The nurses were superb and my parents, friends in San Francisco, and my common-law girlfriend all gave me fantastic support and were tremendous. Her mother was and continues to be a wonderful, caring, devoted, and loyal woman. She visited me every single day when I was in the hospital.

Burns are painful, but I have little recollection of that part of the recovery process. Although my hands were different and I had challenges, I was still fully functional. The burns changed my appearance, so much so that I once had children in a playground yell "Monster, Monster" as I passed by them.

I learned to do things again, slowly, and within two years had gone back to flying airplanes. I decided a move was in order, so in 1973, my girlfriend and I moved to Crested Butte, Colorado which was a Shangri-La in the Rockies. We bought a house together but I was pretty much a jerk to her. She was the lightning rod for my anger and frustration, and as a result, she decided to move to Seattle.

On November 11, 1975, I was planning to fly my Cessna to San Francisco. Shortly after taking off my plane stalled because it had not been completely de-iced. It smashed belly first into the runway and the crash left me paralyzed from the waist down.

The crash was tougher to take than the motorcycle accident, because ultimately paralysis is much more limiting than burns. I recovered in a progressive hospital that allowed me some flexibility. The typical patient was a teenager who got drunk, did not wear a seatbelt and then was in a car accident. At least when I was paralyzed, I was older and had been through one big bump already. I understood that I was not being sent to jail or being locked up, and that the people in the hospital were working for me and not the other way around. It was important for us to understand that we were able to function socially. Some guys were my age and we went out to bars in town and had fun. I even arranged a Super Bowl party in our ward, complete with beer. Within three or four months I was up and running my life again.

I was finagled into serving out a vacancy on the Crested Butte town council. I had not wanted to do this, because I was preparing to move to a warmer climate and being on the town council would cut into my flexibility. There was a mountain behind Crested Butte with a molybdenum mineral deposit and a mining company saw a huge profit potential in it. One day I was driving with a fellow councilman, who was running for the $25-a-month job of mayor, and we got talking about the mining company. He felt no one could stop the company and that they would do what they wanted, so the town should try to broker the best deal possible.

Hearing that was like the gauntlet being thrown down. It had been two years since the plane crash. My life told me there was another way and that I should battle the mining company by running for mayor of Crested Butte. I was well known in the community, and ran a tough campaign, winning by twenty votes. We defeated the mining company.

I next ran for Congress but was defeated. I had spent a lot of money on the campaign, and was now running out of money. I needed to get an income-producing job, so I started hosting a talk show and doing the beginnings of some television work, which was interesting since I was not the typical blow-dried host, yet I was comfortable in front of the camera. I later moved into public speaking and have enjoyed connecting with audiences ever since.

I love the quote, "When one door closes, another opens but too often we spend our time looking at the closed door for so long that we never see the open one." Life often looks like nothing but closed doors because we do not have the flexibility to see the open doors.

No absolute relationship exists between any two variables. For instance, short fingers and looking unusual does not automatically equal disaster, end of world, go hang yourself. Nor does winning the lottery, looking like Brad Pitt, and having six Rolls Royce's equal lifetime happiness. The bottom line is that we really do have the power to choose how we react to these events. We have a huge say in how we perceive things and are limited or not limited by things.

If you screw up, recognize it is fine because it certifies that you are a member of the human race!

The world may dump garbage on me and it may not be my fault, but I still am completely responsible for me. The question is am I going to change, or just wait for help? I accept that not everything can be fixed by only ourselves and that in some instances, professional help is needed. Many people spend their lives feeling that someone else has to fix their lives for them. It's not what happens to you, it's what you do about it.

Tony Robbins said it best when he said, "If you do not like where you are, then go where it feels different, looks different, and the people are different. Get up and move and things will change. You will then have different inputs and the ability to see things in a different light."

Before I was paralyzed, there were 10,000 things I could do; now there are 9,000. I can either dwell on the 1,000 I have lost, or focus on the 9,000 I have left.

****

W Mitchell has survived and persevered through two enormous personal tragedies. Today he helps people through speeches, tapes, and books by delivering his message "Take Responsibility For Change."

CHAPTER TWENTY-FOUR

TERRY-JO MYERS

I would not have cared if I had killed myself or anyone in my way.

****

Terry-Jo Myers is a professional golfer who was diagnosed in 1983 with interstitial cystitis, a bladder disease that is estimated to affect over 700,000 Americans.

As an amateur, she was a five-time winner of the Southwest Florida Junior Golf Association Championship as well as the Southwest Florida Women's Amateur. She continued her golf career at Florida International University.

Terry-Jo joined the Ladies Professional Golf Association (LPGA) in 1986. Despite excruciating pain from interstitial cystitis, for thirteen years she played more than twenty tournaments per year (except in 1989, when she gave birth to her daughter, Taylor-Jo). She collected her first victory on the tour in 1988 at the Mayflower Classic.

****

A typical week on tour for me consists of a corporate outing on Monday in a separate city from where the tournament will be played. That same evening I fly to the city where the tournament site is and play a practice round on Tuesday and a pro-am on Wednesday. The tournament starts on Thursday and goes to Sunday, unless I miss the cut and in which case I have a weekend off. On Sunday evening I fly to a new city and repeat the process. On average I am at the course for eight to ten hours per day.

I was born in Fort Myers, Florida on July 23, 1962, and started playing golf when I was about six years old. I was encouraged by my mother who was a tremendous athlete and club champion at three different golf courses. I also played tennis, but to me, golf was the only sport. Ever since I was a little girl, a golf career was all I wanted. I loved the solitude and could stand on the range for hours feeling the clubface hitting the ball.

In August of 1983, just before my senior year, I had a searing pain in my bladder. I was told I had interstitial cystitis, which is a painful bladder condition. There was very little research on it and there was no cure for the disease. At age twenty-one, I was told, "You will just have to learn to live with it." Those words still echo through my head because it is probably the worst thing I have ever been told.

About 10% of interstitial cystitis cases are chronic like mine. 20% have more frequent flares and 70% only flare once every month or two. My case resulted in my having to urinate up to 40-50 times per night every night. For eleven years I never slept at night. The frequency of urination was the same in the day. It felt like there were paper cuts lining my bladder wall, and when urine hit the wall, the pain was intense. I cringed if anyone got within three feet of me because my body hurt so much and I feared someone bumping into me.

The "knife in the back" feeling I experienced when I injured my back in 1998, cannot compare to interstitial cystitis, which is ten times more painful. With back pain, if you fall asleep you will stay asleep for a bit, whereas with interstitial cystitis I could not sleep. If I was around my friends and they told a joke and I laughed, I would quickly feel the pain in my bladder and stop laughing.

Despite playing on the tour, I did not concentrate on golf. I missed countless short putts and probably had the worst putting average because my focus was on getting to the next port-o-john or bathroom. I absolutely was the fastest person on tour, because I had to get to that bathroom. I kept my condition secret and only a handful of times did a fellow player mention that I was going a lot.

I felt like a prisoner when I was far from a bathroom. To escape, I used to bodybuild, sometimes spending up to four hours in the gym. The pain from working out that hard would temporarily mask the agony. I made a big mistake by trying to live with the pain and I did not tell anyone except for my immediate family for many years. At times I wanted to scream, "Help me, I know I have a name for the disease but I do not know what to do about it."

My husband and I started to date when I was a senior in high school, and in 1987, we were married. We had our only child in 1989. He was the lightning rod for my anger and I was verbally abusive to him. Fortunately my career took me away from him for three weeks at a time. During that period, being away from home was better than being there. A lot of trust and faith is required to have a successful marriage with a golf partner because you are apart for long stretches of time. He has been very faithful and an incredible inspiration. If I were him, I would have left me long ago.

I wanted to take my life hundreds of times. More than once, I was driving dangerously at over 100 miles per hour on an interstate trying to get to a washroom at a rest area and not caring if I killed myself or anyone in my way. That was the mindset I was in.

I did not always have a positive attitude, and my faith wavered through the process. I would cry out to God and say, "What are you teaching me, what do I need to learn from this?" I would tell myself, "You cannot be angry or depressed. You must be strong and persevere and at the end you will discover why you went through it." I had enough faith to believe there was a purpose in this ordeal and to bring myself back from low points.

When the pain took over, I was not in the right frame of mind. Those times I put the disease ahead of everything in my life. Other times I was stronger and would put God in control and say, "I will live and I will get through it no matter how long it takes."

My mother was my rock. I absolutely looked up to her. She helped me to understand both the Bible and faith beyond religion. There were times I was on the bathroom floor just wanting to die because I was in so much pain. Despite seeing this, she would never allow me to say, "Why me?" She was always there for me and relentless in her message to love others, learn, and serve.

For so many years I used golf to keep myself alive. If it had been taken away from me because of my health, then the disease would have won. My marriage could have failed or other things could have happened, but they would not have had the impact of my career ending. It was the last thing I was clinging to.

I finally started to understand the effect the disease was having on my life when I met Dr. Bill Evans. He asked me how difficult it was to keep my marriage together, how I could travel, and how tough it was to be a mother with interstitial cystitis. I did not realize until that point that the disease was affecting and destroying all the other aspects of my existence.

In 1994, I went public with interstitial cystitis. My peers on tour were incredibly supportive when I finally told them. They said to me, "Why did you not tell us? We would have been there for you." I kept it a secret because I had my "gameface" on. When you are an athlete you do not want to show anyone if you are in pain or not feeling well. It is amazing and powerful what your mind will do to let you accomplish something.

Elmiron is a drug that in 1995 made me symptom-free. It took five months for it to kick in and repair the bladder wall. I could see that a breakthrough year was coming because for the first time since college, I could once again concentrate and focus on golf. To have fun again so many years later was wonderful.

I believe the reason I went through it is to help others by publicizing and educating people about the disease. It is not easy for me to talk about it, because in order to tell the truth, I must go so deep into my personal life and remember things I would prefer to forget. Emotionally it tears me apart, and I am drained after a talk. But if I allow myself to forget what I went through then I haven't learned my lesson, which is to take things one day at a time.

The key for me is to keep my priorities in check and to make sure faith is the leading one. I have learned through my fight with interstitial cystitis that life is truly a blessing. We all have a responsibility to teach others from our own experiences. Most of the toughest battles are the greatest lessons taught. You shouldn't keep those lessons to yourself!

****

In late 1995, after eleven years of suffering and agony caused by interstitial cystitis, Terry-Jo became symptom-free. Two years later she had a breakthrough year and won two tournaments, earning over $300,000 and ranking 22nd of all professional golfers that year.

Since 1998, she has had two operations to repair herniated discs, but has battled back and resumed playing on the tour.

CHAPTER TWENTY-FIVE

RICHARD SAMMONS

I had completely lost my sight.

****

Richard Sammons was born February 1, 1929, with a condition called retinitis pigmentosa that caused him to gradually lose his vision.

****

One of my first jobs was working at the theater in town but I was not very good at helping people find seats because my vision was so poor in the dark that I could not tell whether the seat was occupied.

I joined the military and was in the army when the Korean War started. I was assigned to the signal corps and arrived in Korea in 1953, the last year of the war. We were responsible for the installation, operation, and maintenance of communications. I never fired a rifle at anyone. The worst it got for me was when we were under artillery barrage.

In 1952, I married and had two sons born in 1954 and 1958. After the war, we moved to Corpus Christi, Texas and I ended up working at Burroughs Corporation where I got on the job training while working with Mainframe computers. I stayed there for twenty plus years.

In early 1970, my eyesight started to deteriorate. I was only forty years old. Things were getting blurry and harder to see, and I was diagnosed with retinitis pigmentosa. Unrelated to my vision problems, my marriage was unraveling, and we divorced in 1972. My vision degenerated over the next ten years. I had four car accidents in the last year I worked for Burroughs as I was not seeing as I should. Luckily, the only damage from the mishaps was a few scars.

As a result of my driving problems, I started to ride my bicycle to work and relied on my hearing to avoid accidents. Unfortunately, a car hit me while I was on my bike. It was my fault. The lady who was driving was just about scared to death. I felt it was not fair for me to be out there, so I put in for disability retirement in 1980 at age 51. At that point, I had completely lost my sight. It was frustrating to figure out how to do things with no vision and I had a fear of what the future would hold.

The Veterans administration talked me into going to university. I really enjoyed the studying. They had no facilities for disabled people at that time. I would record the lessons and type my notes. Tests were taken by having someone read to me and then I would type my answers on the computer. I got my Bachelors degree in Sociology in 1990 at the University of Texas in Brownsville and later earned my Masters in English.

I came up to Minnesota in 1998, for a 50th high school reunion and the experience made me realize that I wanted to move back there. At the reunion, I met a lady I used to go to school with. We talked, wrote letters, and when I came up for a vacation, we got married. It was the worst mistake I have ever made. It didn't last at all, and financially, I was a lot worse off after the marriage, because I paid many of her debts. I now feel that the best companion for me is my closest friend who is a black Labrador seeing-eye dog.

My friends got me involved with Lifetime Learning, which provides education mainly for people over the age of fifty. I was asked by them to make a computer lab viable for the blind. We applied and received various grants that allowed us to buy two computer systems.

One student I had was 86 years old. She used a walker to get around, and had just bought herself a computer. She asked me, "Am I too old to learn?" I told her that we are only too old to learn when we think we can't.

I have also trained people that can afford computers at home. One student, a doctor, told me he could not learn because he could not type. I said, "Doc, you are eating with a fork and knife—it is that easy." Now he is on the Internet and thinks it is the greatest thing in the world!

I have become fairly active in the church. It is nearby, and I can go over in the week on my own for different events. I have met a wonderful group of people there. The Thursday before Easter, I walked a couple of blocks in the dark to the evening service at the church. The lady behind me asked, "How did you get over here in the dark all alone?" I laughed and replied, "I am always in the dark."

What I miss the most about not having my sight are the looks on people's faces. I have never really seen my grand-daughter's and grandson's facial expressions. When she was a little girl, my granddaughter would jump on my lap so I could Braille her smile. Blindness is more of a nuisance than a disability. The hardest part is to overcome the beliefs of sighted people who think it is more of a problem than it is.

Many people who develop a disability have trouble admitting they need help. You have to be aware that you cannot do everything and not be afraid to ask for help. What happens to you in life is not important. What is important is how you handle it. You can let adversity knock you down and destroy your life, or you can accept it.

Focus on what you can do and then work harder at those things.

****

It is estimated that there are over 10 million blind and visually impaired people in the United States of which roughly 13% of that total are legally blind.

Instead of sitting back after being forced to retire at age 51, Richard went back to university and completed two degrees. He has since devoted his time to helping others with visual handicaps and was featured in Minnesota's largest newspaper as an "Ageless Hero" award winner for his volunteer efforts, as selected by Blue Cross.

CHAPTER TWENTY-SIX

DIANE MACWILLIAMS

The business was in terrible shape and should have been forced into bankruptcy. We had to decide whether or not to close it.

****

Diane MacWilliams is an entrepreneur, who with her husband, founded Quicksilver Associates, to provide creative talents to help enterprises develop special effects in slides and graphics.

****

I first encountered how tough it would be for a woman to make it in the business world after graduating from the University of Illinois with a Bachelor of Arts degree in Fine and Applied Arts. I was working as a designer in the audiovisual department of Arthur Andersen and Company. My chauvinistic boss told me to expect a small raise after my first year. The men got larger raises and his justification was that they needed more money to take women out on weekends. I decided I did not need to work for him, and even though Arthur Andersen and Company were appalled and offered me different jobs, I thought it was time to look for something more enjoyable and closely related to my interests.

I met my business partner, Bill, while he owned a small struggling ad agency. In 1976, we became a couple and opened Quicksilver Associates. We spent twenty-four hours a day together, thinking and talking about the business. We had a great location in downtown Chicago in an old brownstone with a roof garden. People often stopped by after work to listen to music, barbecue, and have a good time. Later that year, Bill and I were married.

The biggest hurdle starting out was money — we had none. We had no hope of getting financing, but luckily, we had a very forgiving landlady who would let us go months before paying our rent and a grocery store that gave us credit. The little money we made on jobs was reinvested in equipment. After a year, we had picked up some major clients like CBS, Quaker Oats, and International Harvester.

Quicksilver took off and we had plenty of work, so we hired several new people. We had no education or background in business, yet money was coming in, so it worked out well. International Harvester became our biggest client requiring most of our time and energy. In the early eighties we had our first experience with a recession and our work with Harvester came to a standstill, which put us in a dire situation. We had just bought a building and were renovating it so we could have space to expand. We had to stop paying ourselves, layoff staff, and hit the pavement to rebuild our client base. Our survival instinct kept us going. We felt we had built a great company, and we were not about to give up.

At the time we had bank financing on the renovation of the building. As the recession deepened, our banker wanted us to sell out. I believe he did not have faith that a creative services company owned by a woman could survive.

Another time, an insurance guy would not sell me insurance because he assumed I was the secretary. It was still very much a "man's world" in the 80s. Luckily, dealing with a woman wasn't a problem to our clients.

I became pregnant in 1982, and delivered a boy, Russell, on Superbowl Sunday. The next day he became very ill. He lacked an amino acid called arginine, which removed ammonia from his system. He slipped into a coma and had seizures before a treatment was determined. Russell finally came home after a month in the hospital. His health became a life and death battle because it was so hard to regulate his medicines and he had sustained brain damage from the seizures.

I went back to work, but often, I would be in the middle of something with a client, and then get a call saying Russell had to go to the emergency room. I was lucky that I had assistants who could step in and carry things forward, and clients who were very supportive.

It was terrible seeing Russell go through this illness. I was under so much stress, I do not even remember parts of my life or people from that period. I put all my energy into Russell, and drew strength from him. He had so much love and would laugh and giggle when he was healthy. He taught me that what was important about life was to enjoy it because it is a special gift never to be taken for granted.

In 1987, Russell's health became very unstable. He was very sick and he had already been in the hospital for the month of October. On a Monday night in November, I was getting ready to spend the night in the hospital. Earlier that day the doctor tried to insert a central line in his chest but they couldn't make it work. His veins had all collapsed and his skin was falling off. I went down to get a coke and saw a chapel that I had not noticed before. I went in and I prayed that God would take him and stop him from suffering. I knew he would go somewhere where he could feel better. When I walked out of the chapel, they were paging me. Russell had died. As a result, I truly believe there is a God who answers your prayers and who you can talk to anytime.

For five years, our lives had been built around trying to keep Russell alive and doing everything we could to enjoy our time with him. I felt like I was sinking into a black hole for a year, and I did not know if I would come up. I was very sad and I hurt tremendously.

During Russell's life I had been given the opportunity to help start the Chicago chapter of the Make-A-Wish Foundation. I visited hospitals at night and saw what other children and parents were going through. I met so many children who needed the hope and joy that a wish could bring them. It was very inspiring getting to know kids with incredible courage and great attitudes despite the fact that their lives would be short. Working with the Make-a-Wish Foundation was a great way to deal with the grief of Russell's death because it was his life that allowed me to help get this chapter started and now others would benefit from it. He left a wonderful legacy.

Time helped the healing process. Within the next year, we adopted a son, and then found out I was pregnant. My adopted son was born in 1988, and our daughter was born in 1989. At that time, I had taken a year off from the business, and felt that "Whatever happens to the business, happens." My children were exactly nine months apart so I had my hands full. I really enjoyed that year with my two babies.

In my absence, my husband had been running Quicksilver. When I returned, it was in terrible shape and should have been forced into bankruptcy. Another recession had begun and most of the clients we had were gone. We had to decide whether or not to close it. I brought in a friend, Hal, who had an accounting background and he helped by auditing and going through our financial records for two months.

My husband quit the business around 1990, and soon after he left our marriage as well. We were divorced in 1992, and it was very tough because we had been married for fifteen years. My parents had been married for fifty years and I could not imagine that our relationship would have been any different. To get through it, I drew upon the friendship and support of other people.

I started selling again, and Hal became the controller and my business partner. It was overwhelming at first, with all the changes in computers, but also very interesting. It was an exciting time, because due to the growth of the dotcom companies, the opportunities to expand our creative work were endless, and often within very tight deadlines. Our business increased in scope and size. After twenty years, I knew our business was a survivor.

Hal died in 1998, of AIDS. The last year of his life he was very sick, and was using his job, which he loved, for his will to live. I needed to let him do that, but he was not keeping up and again the accounting part of the business wasn't being managed. Luckily we were so busy that there was money to pay the bills. A small business has a human side, and being there and supporting your people means as much as anything else. I know Hal would have done the same for me.

It is a challenge being a parent and running a company. You want the best for everybody, and as the president, I realize that I could drive myself crazy if I push too hard for there are unlimited opportunities to work around the clock to accomplish all that needs to be done. I am home at least three nights a week on time, and have a housekeeper who helps out, too. Their father assists as well, and we have a friendly relationship. My children keep me sane and inspire me to be the best that I can.

The key to doing well is being flexible and knowing that good and bad times come and go. When times are good you still have to be conservative because they won't last forever and when times are bad you have to persevere and believe you can get through it.

I have had a fantastic life. I have wonderful kids and great relationships with people through the business, Make-A-Wish, and the community that I live in. Though there have been hurdles, most of my life has been very positive. Seeing all the people who help Make-A-Wish by giving time or resources to make a wish come true makes me feel that if we can each do a little bit more for others in need, then we would have a much better world.

The tough periods come and go, and you have to be patient, because losing sleep and getting angry will do no good at all. Think logically and you can get through anything.

You need to look at each day as a special gift because life is very short.

****

Diane MacWilliams won the 2001 Woman Business Owner of the Year award as presented by the National Association of Women Business Owners, and as well, has been inducted into the Chicago Area Entrepreneurial Hall of Fame. In 2002, she was named the Illinois Small Business Person of the Year by the United States Small Business Administration.

Quicksilver Associates has evolved over the years with technology, and has survived three economic slumps. On June 6, 2003, it celebrated its twenty-seventh anniversary.

CHAPTER TWENTY-SEVEN

FRANK O'DEA

I was living on the streets panhandling for money, staying at fifty-cent flophouses, and struggling to get through each day.

****

Frank O'Dea hit rock bottom at age 26. His life since then, has been nothing short of remarkable.

****

I was born June 14, 1945 in Montreal, Quebec, the second oldest of four children. My home life was typical, yet for reasons I do not completely understand, I was an angry young man, full of fear and with low self-confidence.

I started to drink at an early age, stealing liquor from our home for weekends. Alcohol somehow gripped me in a way that led to more serious problems. At age sixteen, I was arrested for impaired driving, and a spree of drinking occurred that resulted in my wrecking several cars and failing out of high school. To finance this lifestyle, I even stooped to writing "bad" cheques.

My father was tired of my continual drinking and by the violent behavior that the alcohol fueled. He threw me out of the house, hoping that it might be a wake-up call for me to get my life in order. I moved to Toronto, Ontario to start a new life but I was still lonely and lacking confidence in my abilities. I attempted but failed to hold various sales positions. Alcohol was becoming the lead value in my life. All activity revolved around the bottle, and it led to a quick progression downwards.

Binge drinking consumed my money, and my car was repossessed. The landlord of a small apartment where I was living changed the locks and I found myself homeless, without money, and an alcoholic at age 26. With two friends from the street, I started a life of panhandling and dreaming unrealistically of what I would do in the future.

On the morning of December 23, 1971, I had a moment of clarity. There was no magical "one thing" but just a confluence of circumstances that led to a crashing con-clusion. It was too many nights on park benches, too many nights running from the cops, too many lies, too many, too many. It was apparent that alcohol and I did not mix. I said, "enough" and threw in the towel, for it was either die or change. I recalled an ad I had heard for alcohol recovery while borrowing five dollars from Isadore (Izzie) Reingewertz, a former customer whom I had sold paint products to.

That day I met with a group of people who shared my challenge. The first meeting confirmed I had made the right decision, and with the support of Joe, my mentor from the program, and Izzie, I slowly began to piece together a new life away from drinking. I initially worked full time for Izzie and leaned heavily on Joe. After four months of my staying dry, Joe purchased a second-hand suit for me, and within a short period, I had found a job selling cleaning equipment.

To change a negative value, in my case alcohol, you need support and you must be ready to try and change. I was 51% sure that I did not want to drink again. I built on this and today I am 100% sure.

Initially I was trying to do everything at once, and trying to turn impossible dreams into reality. In a way, I was hoping to overcome the previous twenty-seven years of my life with one quick move. I started to realize that change did not come that quickly, and that it would take smaller successes that built on each other.

In 1972, I reconnected with my family. It was awkward and difficult, and there was a lot of suspicion. It was not a "prodigal son" type of return, as I had made many promises in the past to them that I had not kept. They chose to sit back and watch to see if I was serious about my turnaround. I went back to help my two drinking friends from two years earlier, and found that one had died, and the other person was unready to admit his life needed changing. It was sad and very frustrating.

The emotions that had controlled me, such as guilt, fear, and loneliness, were starting to disappear. It took a while for the self-respect to come back. I can remember one day selling when I was too frightened to even get out of my car and call on a customer. I managed to upgrade my job to selling larger dollar products, and for the first time in my life I saved $1000 in a Canada Savings Bond.

In 1974, I became the campaign manager for the federal Liberal party in the riding of Halton, Ontario. I developed a friendship with the campaign finance chairman, Tom Culligan, and we decided to form a partnership after we were successful in getting our candidate elected. Following a couple of attempts at business that yielded insignificant results, we undertook the running of a coffee kiosk in a large mall. We sold related coffee products as well, and called the stand The Second Cup.

Our lack of experience in the coffee business became very apparent when we were informed by a new employee that the brown paper sacks that contained four types of coffee we had purchased from a discount supplier were, in fact, all the same type of Colombian. At first the business struggled, but over the next six years, we managed to sell over one million cups of coffee, as well as tons of coffee beans.

Recently, I went into a Second Cup at 11 o'clock at night and as I looked around, I saw that the average person was in their late teens. When I was that age there was nowhere to go, so by creating the stores, maybe we also contributed to a safe environment for kids to go to at night.

I was on a flight to Florida on a winter night in 1988 and had run out of reading material. As a last resort, I started to talk to the man beside me. His name was Peter Daglish and he was coming back from Ethiopia, where he had worked with street children, of which 23% were carrying the AIDS virus. We discussed how one could educate these children of third world countries, and as the plane landed we concluded that we would make an animated film to do this. This project led to the creation of a charity, Street Kids International.

We raised $2.5 million dollars, and garnered support from some of the best animators in the business. A film was produced which was described as an educational primer for the 21st century. More importantly, it has now been translated into 23 different languages, and shown to millions of viewers.

When in trouble, you must find someone to talk to, whether that is a recovery group, a therapist, friends or family. It is much easier having others working with you. It is also essential to deal with your problems and then move on. Don't live in the past, blaming others.

Faith used to play a large role for me, but it has slipped in the last few years due to the focus on raising children and a lack of time. I think of faith today as spirituality, and I want to reconnect with it.

Take responsibility for your life. When you say yes to life, the potential for complete change is very near the surface. I was not aware of that and most of us are not. Life happens, and because it does, it takes us to all kinds of places that we could not have planned. There is nothing wrong with planning, but always leave yourself flexible to life's events.

For the past twenty-five years, I have known that starting and managing businesses is the direction I want to take in my life, but I did not always know the road to achieving success for me. Your vision may take you on roads you cannot plan. It's like traveling to California, not being sure how to get there, and just generally heading west.

We all have an internal prism that takes the outside environment and filters it and presents us with how we see the world. Just slightly altering this prism is easy; for example, changing a job, changing a bad habit, etc. When you do, the result is that the outside world will appear to be different, and accordingly, your view of it will change, as well.

I did not know that when I had my first drink it would change my life entirely, or that a guy I met on an airplane would lead to Street Kids International being formed. A dinner I attended in Winnipeg led to the Canadian Landmine Foundation being started.

One small positive change can affect the outcome of your life.

****

According to a 1998 U.S. survey of homelessness in 30 cities, it was found that children under eighteen accounted for 25% of the urban homeless, and that single men comprised 45% of the total. Roughly one quarter suffer from some form of serious mental illness. The number of people who have been homeless at one point in a year range from two million to seven million depending upon the methodology used to do the research. The statistics vary dramatically due to the difficult nature of getting an accurate picture of the problem.

Frank O'Dea started one of Canada's most successful coffee chains: The Second Cup. Expansion and franchising increased the number of outlets to over sixty by 1984, and sales mushroomed to over fifteen million dollars. He sold his shares and purchased ownership of ProShred, a paper shredding company, a move that would also net him a phenomenal return.

Frank has also used his entrepreneurial acumen to start various charities like Street Kids International and most recently the Canadian Landmine Foundation, which is committed to eradicating anti-personnel landmines and ending the human suffering caused by them.

CHAPTER TWENTY-EIGHT

MARY STREAM

I had $100 bills falling all over me, and I rolled in them screaming. It was such a thrill!

****

The financial windfall was short-lived. Mary Stream raised four children by herself after her husband was killed in an automobile accident. Mary's biggest challenge came after her youngest daughter graduated from high school and moved out of their house in Red Wing, Minnesota.

****

My father was a violent alcoholic and I can remember hiding in the back seat of an old car in my pajamas because I had talked back to him. Our family all lived in fear of his violent nature.

I was not confident as a young girl. I was overweight, big busted, and felt that guys only liked me because of my breasts. In my junior year, I became pregnant. The baby's father was forced into the service by his parents, and I left school and took care of people in a Catholic charity home while pregnant. After delivering a baby boy, I was not even allowed to see him and he was put up for adoption.

One year after I graduated from high school, I married a man six years older than me. We had the first of four children the year after in January of 1967. My husband was a carpenter, while I stayed at home and raised our children in a beautiful house on a golf course. We had a good relationship and did lots of family things such as going camping in the summer.

When he turned 36, he started drinking with a new friend who was single, wealthy, and younger. As soon as alcohol came into the picture, I shut down the marriage instantly because I feared it would lead to a situation like the one I had grown up in. I insisted in 1978 that we separate even though he was not doing the negative things my father had. He moved out on a Thursday and the next day when he got paid, he brought over his paycheck. He was so good to the kids and me. He took them any time I wanted and never missed a school program.

In April of the following year, I told him he could have the kids the week of his birthday if he wanted. He replied that he would prefer a family dinner like we used to have. I really missed everything we had before we separated, but I was too afraid I would go back to a relationship and end up living like my mother did, with an alcoholic. As a result, I chose not to get together with him despite his efforts.

Two weeks later, I went out on my first date since our split. Later that same night, he died in a head-on car accident. It was determined he was under the influence of alcohol. It was very devastating. I felt tremendous guilt and shame.

I had been involved in teaching Sunday school and getting my kids to church, but I lost all faith in God when my husband died. I could not understand why a loving God would take this man and leave awful men and husbands on the earth.

My children were five, eight, ten, and twelve when he died. I focused on being a good mother for I knew that I was all my kids had. I went to every football game and track meet. The sign in the back of my car said, "Mom's taxi." When they finally grew up and started to leave home, I felt that no one needed me, and I had no purpose. I had lost my identity because everything I did involved my kids.

I started gambling in 1989, when my youngest daughter was a senior at high school. I found that when I gambled nothing bothered me. It was like a good drug. It was all that I could think about, and it was comforting. I also started to work in a casino. I realized I had a problem when I started bouncing checks. For a little while I did get things under control and I watched my gambling closely.

One day, a couple of boarders paid their rent and I took $100 of it to the casino. I started on the blackjack table and won $150. I then went to a red, white, and blue dollar machine and I hit $120 on the first pull. Next, I went around the corner to another machine and hit red 7's and won $5000. The casino did not ask if I wanted cash or a check. They just came back and gave me a stack of fifty $100 bills.

I went home, and as I was about to make the bed, I took the money out and threw it up to the ceiling and watched $100 bills fall all over me. It was such a thrill! I was literally rolling in the money like some kind of nut. Over the next few weeks, I gambled very little and did responsible things like paying bills. I had worked so hard all my life, since I was eleven. I felt that this was my reward for years of hard work.

The feeling of excitement of my big win was still in my head when, three weeks after I won that money, the casino I worked at opened up gambling to employees. As a cocktail waitress, even if I had no money, I would earn tips of $80-100 and use that as my gambling money. I tried to avoid gambling by not bringing a change of clothes to work because rules did not allow me to gamble in a cocktail uniform. I would get around this by going to the gift shop and buying new clothes, or I would wear my coat over my uniform. It was crazy. I never felt so out of control in my life.

I stopped paying bills. Twice I got six months behind on house payments. I did not realize I was so far behind on payments as the gambling had taken over so much. I only responded to emergency notices that threatened to turn my power off. To support my habit, I refinanced my house seven times and the house payments went from $225 a month to $998 a month.

If somebody had told me that I would stay awake for 36 hours, not eat and only drink coffee and smoke cigarettes, I would not have believed it. It was nuts. In 1993, I gambled just about every day. I was under severe financial stress and my work started to suffer. The casino fired me on January 1, 1994.

I told a counselor provided by the casino about my gambling. He suggested that I go to Minneapolis where there was a very intense outpatient program for addicted gamblers. I attended four days a week, for three or four hours per night. There was a small group of five or six of us and we discussed our problems, and learned more about our addiction.

It was really hard, especially since I drove by three casino exits on the way to Minneapolis. There were days I would pull my car off the road and bawl, or times I would take the exit to the casino, and somehow gather the strength and then turn around. I knew I could never let myself gamble again.

At one point, I had even thought of driving my car off a road at a spot where there was a steep drop. When I later told my son, he asked me, "How could you ever think of doing that after Dad died in a car accident?" That was the furthest thing from my mind at that time. I never even thought of my kids reaction.

After I stopped gambling, I went on a mission to try to save my house. I put too much effort into it, and refinanced at 18% interest. I finally realized it was only a house and let it go in 1996, but it was very tough to do, because I felt like it was all I had.

My children were excellent and a great support group. They were all living their lives throughout the country when my addiction was at its worst. My son moved back in with me when I quit and he took over my finances.

The Gamblers Anonymous group became my faith. A person who had quit around the same time I did started hanging out with me and she would stay at my place after the Friday meeting until Sunday just so neither of us would gamble. Within a year, I had started a Gamblers Anonymous meeting in Red Wing and soon after that, I started sponsoring people.

I never did remarry and in retrospect, I wish my husband and I had stayed together. After some time, my faith returned stronger than ever and it has since helped keep me strong. The forgiving God I know and love suffered a lot for us.

I believe that we each have a purpose and a different thing to do on this earth. We also need to forgive ourselves. I have to look back on the toughest times with some sense of humor. The last person to forgive me for my mistakes was me.

If I ever forget the pain of my addiction, then I risk going back to it.

****

Between 2% and 6% of adults are addicted to gambling. Although males tend to be more at risk, an increasing percentage of females are joining recovery programs. The impact of gambling addictions in society is reflected through increased legal, medical, and social costs. Crime is higher because of gambling. Two thirds of individuals with gambling issues have admitted to committing illegal acts.

It is estimated that problem and pathological gamblers provide over a third of the revenue of casinos. States and provinces are relying more and more on taxes generated by casinos and, as additional sites open, the negative effects of gambling will be amplified.

One source of assistance for the problem is Gamblers Anonymous. It is an organization where men and women share their experiences and help others to recover. The only requirement to belong is that each member desires to stop gambling.

Today, Mary Stream helps others who are facing the same challenges that she has overcome.

CHAPTER TWENTY-NINE

JOHN STEER

I lay for two days under dead bodies before I was finally rescued.

****

John Steer experienced two of the worst battles in the Vietnam War.

****

My father was a truck driver, a tough guy, and a drunk. If he said something, he would stand by it. He never backed down, which is a trait that I probably inherited from him. Mother was a sweet lady who was only nineteen when she was married. Frequently, she was verbally put down by my father. She was a beaten woman who lacked confidence to make it on her own.

I remember one day when my father went ballistic because a teacher was going to hold me back a year when I was in second grade. For over an hour, he slapped me and screamed, "Read, you dumb s.o.b." Likely as a result of his abuse, I still hate to read to this day.

Memories of my early years were of bouncing from school to school and having to fight to prove myself, because the schools were in tough areas. I was constantly in fights and had absolutely no self-esteem. I left home at age fifteen. My uncle tried to get me into the navy at age seventeen but, without a diploma and having a juvenile criminal record, it was a no go. I finally got a waiver from a judge and Dad signed for me to go into the army.

I did fairly well in basic and advanced training and loved the competition. I was beginning to feel that I was a somebody and not just some scumbag. My fellow soldiers and I had a lot of pride and confidence in each other.

In March of 1967, I went over to Vietnam. I was a paratrooper with the 173rd Airborne Infantry. I was in small firefights where lives were lost, but they did not compare in magnitude to my first major battle on June 22, at The Slope (*Dak To*), where we lost 78 out of 100 men. I felt responsible at the time for one man getting killed, even though in retrospect I should not have. The hatred and anger that came as a result of this horrible battle changed me. After that, I wanted to kill and die because I felt guilty to be alive.

For the next five months I was a very hateful individual. I was not nice to newly arrived soldiers because I felt they were going to die. I did some awful things and now have trouble comprehending how I was ever that way.

We could not drink in Vietnam, although, I would have drank a gallon of alcohol if we could have gotten it. Occasionally they would bring in two cans of beer per man. I smoked pot about a dozen times. Our unit was out in the field most of the time, and I did not dare to get high because I did not want to compromise my buddies. We had great camaraderie, and I would have rather died than let someone down.

In the jungle, the smells were awful because the dead bodies bloated. In my throat I could taste rotting and burning flesh. The temperature was high, and there were millions of flies. To this day, the smell of fresh cut grass and steamy days bring back memories.

In November 1967, our battalion was given the task of taking Hill 875. My friend Carlos and I volunteered to try an ambush of the North Vietnamese (N.V.) to allow the others in our company time to dig in. The N.V. charged us, but we held our ground and were credited with killing twenty people. I was shot in the back twice and Carlos died across my legs when he was shot in the head. He was posthumously awarded a Congressional Medal of Honor for his actions that day.

Many memories were blocked out around that time. After Carlos died, a man called Kelly came over and intentionally knocked me down and had me crawl up the hill, which saved me, as I would probably have died fighting the N.V. because I was so crazy after Carlos death. As I started to crawl, Kelly threw grenades behind us. We met up with some other members of the company and fought our way up the hill. To this day, I do not know if Kelly survived Vietnam, but I suspect he did not or I likely would have heard about him.

I was in the center of the area where we were positioned. We had run out of water, ammunition, and morphine. We would send out three guys when supplies were dropped by our forces, but they were suicide missions, as the N.V. would pick them off, and leave the wounded person as bait, to entice us to try another mission to save him.

It was dark when all of a sudden by mistake arc lights (*parachute flares*) lit us up and the enemy shot up the wounded under the lighting. Then American jets came and by mistake we were bombed. I was lying with a poncho over my face to cover the glare from the lights, when a 550 pound bomb went off in a tree above me and the last I remember, it was raining bodies and parts of bodies. When I woke, I was nauseated and blood was gushing out of my nose, mouth, and ears. My right arm was gone and my right leg just about off. I lay for two days under dead bodies before I was finally rescued. I had fear at that point and prayed, "God, please do not let me go to hell." I did not ask to go to heaven, only to not go to hell.

Recovering in the field hospital, I remember being afraid to open my eyes. I finally got the courage to do so and saw a little Red Cross worker sitting beside me. She jumped up and was really excited that I was conscious. All of a sudden I was back in reality. My right arm was stretched out in traction, and a sheet stretched tight from my waist out. I asked, "Do I still have my right leg?" and she said, "Yes sir but they are talking about amputating it." The next thing that hit me was, "Thank God I'm alive."

A few days later, I did a press interview at the hospital, and I unloaded my anger, and said, among other things, that it was so stupid trying to take that hill knowing we were vastly outnumbered. I was very angry that my friends were dead. I was later told the tape was confiscated and never played in the United States.

At first, I wanted to be dead because all my friends had died but then I thought, if I start complaining that I am alive, then they ought to get out of their graves and kick me in the butt. I spent two years in hospitals and lost 60 pounds in Vietnam from dysentery.

Upon returning home, I met my future wife, Donna, at a nightclub in Denver. She, like myself, was from Minnesota and I liked it that she did not seem affected by the hook, which was where my arm used to be. We fell in love and got married July 6, 1968.

For many years I suffered from guilt and nightmares. In one breath I would thank God that I was alive, and in the other breath I would scream at God in a rage usually after I had been drinking. I finally let it go and in 1972, I prayed to Jesus and asked him to come into my heart. I began to see all the times I should have been killed. I thought of who had kept me alive, and I repented. The rage and hatred left. I went to my Catholic wife and told her I was saved. She was skeptical at first but over time came to believe it. What impressed her was that I was no longer angry and hateful.

I wrote a book, *Vietnam, Curse or Blessing?*, in 1982. It just about killed me to write it because I had to relive the experience. After I put the book out, I started to get calls from people who were asking for help for themselves or a family member. A prison psychologist, who had enjoyed reading my book, called and asked me to speak to 200 or so Veterans in their prison. The Vets said to me, "Welcome home" and "Thanks for serving our country." I just fell apart and lost it because it was the first time in my life that I had received thanks for being in Vietnam.

They asked me to be their chaplain even though they were a mix of different religions. It was pretty cool. I did that for three years and that opened one door after another to the point where I have been a national chaplain for different organizations and I will probably do twenty veterans reunions this summer. It is amazing to me that someone like myself, with only a 9th grade education, has spoken at colleges and high schools. I think the Lord laid an ambush or something.

Having someone to talk to is important. An understanding wife has helped me tremendously. Groups are good as long as they are not pity parties where someone is trying to tell a worse story than the next person. If you are feeling down, call someone else who is depressed and encourage him or her. Get your eyes off your own problems and look with perspective at the world.

Thousands of others have gone through similar trials to whatever you're facing and with the help of God they are making it one day at a time. My greatest joy is seeing other people come around because of him being in their hearts. It is wonderful that God can take a person like me and help me to feel successful. No longer do I feel I have to prove anything.

My life turned around when I found God, and yours can too.

$$**********************************$$

John Steer lost his right arm and was left with a severely damaged leg, both as a result of a battle in Vietnam. He was awarded two Purple Hearts, an army commendation medal with a V for valor, the Bronze Star, and the Silver Star.

After readjusting to society after the war, he became a national chaplain for many Veterans organizations. John and Donna Steer were awarded the 682nd Presidential Point of Light by President Bush in 1992 for founding and operating a shelter and refuge that was dedicated to stabilizing and reconstructing the lives of troubled veterans and their families. Over the eleven years it operated, they took in over seven hundred veterans.

John has become an ordained minister, a Certified Addiction Specialist, and preached in twenty-seven different countries. He is also a recording artist, singing patriotic and gospel songs, and has received three awards for his music.

CHAPTER THIRTY

LESLIE MOUTON

I felt total disbelief upon finding out that I had breast cancer.

****

At age 35, Leslie Mouton discovered a lump in her breast during a self-exam. In October of 2000, she was diagnosed with breast cancer.

She is the anchor of the noon and 6 p.m. telecasts, Monday through Friday for KSAT 12, the San Antonio affiliate for ABC-TV.

****

A regular daily newscast is run like a well-oiled machine. Even when breaking news happens, it looks more chaotic from the outside. It's a crazy business but a lot of fun too. I feel very privileged to be trusted with the responsibility to inform and educate our viewers about what's going on in our community and the world.

Even after I was on camera I doubted whether I would be able to sustain my career. I would record my shows every day and then sit at home, watching and critiquing my performance to see how I sounded, looked and did. I was very insecure and self-critical. It was actually detrimental, because I obsessed over things that the average person did not see and I spent so much time looking to correct little things that I missed the big picture. It is very easy to get sucked into the competitiveness of it. To set myself apart, I learned that I had to be who I was and not someone I was not.

I thought I would never have to worry about cancer until I was in my 50's and 60's. Each month, I did my self-exams but never thought I would find anything. I felt silly and was apologetic when I went to see the doctor thinking the lump would turn out to be nothing. But it turned out that it was cancer.

I took the approach, "What do we do next? Let's kick this thing and move forward." I have to give the credit to God because I believe this is where the strength came from. My faith was crucial to helping me through this ordeal.

I think it is harder on the family of the person with cancer than it is to be the person going through it, because in my mind I was on a mission. The people who love you can only sit back and watch. I had married in 1990 and our daughter was born eight years later. It was very hard for my husband, Tony, because he is a man who wants to solve everything. All he could do was hold my hand and tell me I was beautiful and that he loved me. He never made me feel that our marriage was threatened or that I was less attractive to him despite the physical changes in my appearance.

When I heard my hair was going to fall out I started to cry like a baby. I looked in the mirror and said, "Why am I freaked out about this?" It was because my hair was a huge part of who I was. I had spent a lot of time and money cutting, combing, and styling it. On good hair days I felt good about myself and on bad hair days I felt bad about myself. I couldn't imagine "no-hair" days. I thought that I would be ugly and I even worried about my marriage. I finally realized that I was still me without hair, and that I was still beautiful.

My daughter started to have nightmares and would come into our room many nights but I figured she was only two and would not understand, so I did not bother explaining it to her. But the night before the operation she said the blessing, "Bless this food and allow it to nourish our body and bless Mommy's booby amen." I just about passed out realizing that she knew something was wrong, so I sat down with her and explained everything that was happening. I told her it would be OK and that she would see scary things, like Mommy's hair falling out, and that I would be sick in bed, too. It is important for parents to realize even young children are aware things are happening and that they should be honest with them about what is going on.

I had to go through four rounds of chemo; one treatment every three weeks, and then radiation therapy five days per week for six weeks. I have mammograms and sonograms every six months now, and bloodwork every three months.

Two weeks after my first chemo treatment, my hair was coming out in clumps so I decided to have a hair shaving party. I was going to lose it on my terms and invited my good friends and family over. I came up with the idea to give away memory locks so we put little braids and pink ribbons in my hair, and when we shaved it off, everyone there got one. We had to make it a fun and positive experience because I knew if I was traumatized, then my daughter would be, too. Afterwards she asked, "Can we do it again tomorrow Mommy?"

I was really afraid of having people find out that I had cancer, because I thought it would paint me as fallible and weak. I felt it would ruin my career and I would no longer have a position in the industry. God truly spoke to my heart and gave me the courage to talk about it publicly. At that point, I felt I was in a position to help young women.

It was really hard for me to picture anchoring the news with a wig on, knowing that I would look sick and viewers would see it, too. I decided the best way to stand up for women and show that bald was beautiful was to anchor an entire newscast without my wig. I was apprehensive about what the viewer reaction might be, but I knew it was a statement I wanted to make. The response was overwhelmingly positive.

I never wore my wig except on the air. I walked around the city bald and never covered my head up. I have met some women who could not even take off their wigs in their own houses, which was sad. Tony, my husband of twelve years, shaved his head too and kept it that way every day until my chemo was over. We got a lot of funny looks when we went out with our daughter.

I did not give up the normalcy of my life. Regardless of how terrible I felt, I still worked. I took a few days off after each round of chemo, and then got dressed and went back and did the news because I did not want the cancer to control my life.

Speaking publicly about my situation has been a real blessing because I travel around with cancer, women's, and church groups. Sharing my story and feeling like I am touching lives is a phenomenal feeling. I could never have seen myself doing this. It is overwhelming to me that I can affect lives—little old me! It has been a huge honor and become something that I love to do.

It is very important that all women, including young women, know they are at risk and that every lump should be taken seriously. It is crucial to find it early and know that if you develop breast cancer as a young woman, you are especially at risk to develop an aggressive type.

If you're facing adversity, let go and allow God to help. You can really get through anything. I believe he can make any aspect in your life a blessing if you allow him to do so. Secondly, you have to let your friends and family help. Rely on them for support. Do not take it all upon yourself.

If you have a positive attitude, good things will happen, but if you wallow in self pity, thinking "poor me, poor me," then tomorrow will probably be a terrible day. Don't feel sorry for yourself or let your brain run away with crazy thoughts of the worst that can happen.

One big thing I learned from all this is how precious, un-appreciated, and short life is. We take it for granted. We focus on what is unimportant. Personally, before I found out I had cancer, I wasted a lot of my time at home, going over tape after tape, rewinding and fast forwarding, instead of spending quality time with my precious two-year-old.

We will all die someday and it may happen because of cancer, a car accident, or old age, but it is crucial that people pay attention to the things that matter, and not wait until some tragedy in their life wakes them up. We do not have control over how we die but we do have control over how we live. I think it is really important that we realize that if we had a bad day, we still had a day, and an opportunity to do something great. You can defeat whatever bad things life throws at you.

****

Leslie Mouton chose to fight her battle in the public eye, and to share her experiences, hoping that they would help others facing similar challenges.

October 2003 was the three-year anniversary of her diagnosis and so far there has been no sign of cancer reappearing.

CHAPTER THIRTY-ONE

JIM SMITH*

I looked up at guards with machine guns staring down at me from the thirty-foot high fences. I was pretty sure this was the end.

****

For trafficking heroin, Jim Smith received a prison term to be served in the federal penitentiary.

He was born in Toronto on June 26, 1951 into a family of seven children and started a life in crime before the age of sixteen. He also became addicted to heroin, and began a twenty-five year cycle of drug addiction and trips to prison.

****

In the first ten years of my life, I moved over thirteen times, and was two years later than most people in completing my grade eight education. My father worked in the produce business and my mother in a restaurant. Self-esteem was nonexistent, due to frequent savage beatings at the hands of my father and to my weak performance in school.

As I grew older, I felt increasing hatred from my father and I lived in fear of him. Relations with him deteriorated when my mother told him that another man had conceived me. I started to frequent the streets in order to get away from home and had brushes with the law for theft, break and enter, and minor drug offenses, all before the age of sixteen.

I left home at age sixteen to live with friends and within one year, I took up the use of heroin, followed by LSD, and all other drugs that were available. My first trip to adult prison occurred shortly thereafter when I was apprehended trying to break into a safe. By the end of 1980, I had been in most of the detention centers and municipal jails in the region.

I became a heroin junkie and had a daughter with a woman who was not a serious romance. They moved to British Columbia and lived a transient life, changing names and addresses frequently. I lost track of my daughter as a result.

In 1983, a guy I knew from the street asked me, "Jimmy, can you get me a gram of junk?" He was with a guy I did not know. I'm not sure why I got it for him in front of a stranger but I was caught off guard and it turned out the stranger was an undercover RCMP officer.

I was convicted of heroin trafficking and transferred to the federal penitentiary. The prison had 160 inmates serving life sentences. Looking up at the guards staring down at me from the thirty-foot high fences, I was pretty sure this was the end. I was shackled, handcuffed, bitter, angry, and very depressed. I felt alone and abandoned. Life seemed to have passed me by.

In prison, looking the wrong way, or speaking to the wrong person can lead to a severe beating or worse. In prison, stabbing and pipings (*using steel pipes as a weapon*) happen, not fist fights. I had a couple of run-ins. One time there was a group of bikers who knew I did not like them. I had an altercation with someone in their clique and later, another inmate asked me to get a person, and when I went upstairs he was not there. Instead, these guys were there drinking brew and taking pills. One of the guys came at me, so I made my move and threw him down and the others moved away from me. They went to get the toughest guy.

Later, I was in my cell with the door open, and a guy walked in and called my name. He sucker-punched me as I was washing my face, and we fought. He was called Rock and was doing nine years for blowing a guy's leg off. I went to solitary confinement and got a lecture from a worker at the prison telling me that I was nuts to go after a biker. My mental state of mind at that point was "Kill or be killed."

In tough situations, guys would "check in" which meant you asked the guard to keep you in lockup or to get you transferred to another place. I did not do that; after being released from solitary, I went back out to the yard. The first guy I met was Rock*. He apologized to me, saying he got the wrong story. The original guy that I beat up was whining and apologizing to me as well. In prison, the decision is either to continue the beef or to let it slide. I let it slide. Prison was a series of near confrontations or fights.

I was released back on to the street, and started using heroin again. By 1990, I had been using drugs for over twenty-one years. In prison I had never taken a trades course, and as a result, I was not qualified for many jobs. The only work I had ever done was in construction as a laborer.

I remarried, and on May 20,1992, my second wife gave birth to a son, Zachary. I felt an immediate and over-powering love for my new child, an emotion that had been vacant from me for so many years. The arrival of my son provided a sense of purpose to my existence. Unlike with my daughter, whom I had never seen, I was determined to set an example for my newborn son.

For the first time, I now had a fresh chance to live and do something right. Having the will to change is a must for a heroin junkie, but the chances of relapse are high. I did heroin twice in the 90s, and both times immediately went to rehabilitation centers, and for a change listened and tried to learn from the suggestions and help. Anger management courses helped me get a better grasp of my upbringing in a troubled home and showed me how it impacted my behavior.

Zack's mother and I parted company because she was still using heroin. He was going to be put into foster homes because she could not take care of him, and they would not let an ex-heroin junkie like me have custody. This motivated me to find a way to move from homelessness to a small one-bedroom apartment. I did this by disconnecting from street people and going into rehabilitation. I knew I had to clean up my own act first, and then start with a plan for the future. I have been consistent in reporting to the people who are trying to help me, such as counselors from the John Howard society and each day I do calisthenics.

Since 1995, I have been completely clean of heroin. Avoiding drugs will be a lifelong challenge. My goal is to be someone that Zachary will be proud of so that he will not be embarrassed when other kids ask, "What does your father do?" I have a strong faith, although I do not go to church often. We still say our prayers, and Zack and I talk about God.

I diligently worked with the Children's Aid Society and they made me jump through hoops. For example I had completed two parenting courses, two anger management courses, and had never been late or missed a meeting or a visit with my son. When I went to court, the judge said to me, in front of the lawyers, "I would never even consider you, Mr. Smith, to parent your son as you are carrying around too much excess baggage from your past to be a parent."

I would not give up. My perseverance paid off and I got Zack on June 2, 2000. He had been in foster care because he was having problems in school which no doubt happened because he was away from me and acting up in class for attention. They classified him as having behavioral problems and sent him to a school that had a teacher who specialized in this area. There has not been one incident since he moved in with me. He just received an award from the principal stating what a good student he is!

Finding a reason to love broke the cycle of heroin, robbery, and jail. Coming to grips with the anger from my childhood and putting the past behind me has let me look forward to the future with Zack, which is very motivating. I am aware that it will be a gradual process to get to a better place, and I understand that setbacks will occur. If he was not in my life, I am not sure if I would have tried to rebuild it.

It seems that Zack is the only person in my life that I have truly loved. In the past, I was always waiting to get hurt, so I usually hurt the other person first. Putting the past behind me and finding a motivating force seems simple in words. I feel I can and will be a constant to my son and someone he can always count on through good or bad times. When I think of him, I get the strength and will to succeed.

I think back on all the times I used to be in jail. Just before I got out, my heart and mind were in the right place, but when I got released, I went back to the only place and people I knew. It was really hard to change this behavior. Finding new friends and changing my life was very difficult. I had to set up some support systems for myself to get over the peaks and valleys. They are a necessity for someone in a tough situation. I abide by the motto "have a good attitude to everything, and good things will follow." You have to listen and not think that you are smarter than everyone else. Most importantly, you must have the desire to straighten yourself out and be honest with yourself.

There will be a lot more rough times than positive ones at first, but you have just got to roll with the punches.

****

Today, Jim lives with his son and deals with the challenges of being a single father, which is a vast improvement over where he was ten years before.

*Jim Smith and Rock are both pseudonyms.

CHAPTER THIRTY-TWO

BUCK O'NEIL

You have to learn to "give it up."

****

John Jordan "Buck" O'Neil Junior was born November 13, 1911, in Carrabelle, Florida. He was a skilled baseball player and in 1933 joined his first professional baseball team, the Tampa Black Smokers. Over the next five years, he traveled the country and played baseball for various organizations.

Jim Crow laws were designed to ensure segregation and they were very much in force in the South at that time. Laws ranged from ruling that there should be different schools for white and African-American students to mandating that African-Americans must use separate waiting rooms and washrooms in public facilities. It was not until 1965 when the Voting Rights Act was passed that all citizens were finally allowed to vote.

Baseball was also segregated, but in 1920, Andrew "Rube" Foster formed an organized league, The Negro National League. It started with eight teams, and soon rival leagues were formed.

Buck joined the Kansas City Monarchs in 1938. The Monarchs were the Negro League's equivalent of the New York Yankees, winning four consecutive Negro American League pennants. His baseball career was interrupted for three years when he served in the Philippines during World War Two. Buck became a player/manager in 1948 and stayed with the Monarchs through the 1955 season. Over his career he played in three Negro American League All-Star games, and two Negro American League World Series.

Jackie Robinson broke the color barrier in baseball when he was signed by the Brooklyn Dodgers. After integration of the Major Leagues began in 1947, the Negro leagues began to lose some of their most talented young players, future hall of fame players like Hank Aaron and Ernie Banks. By the 1960's, the last Negro baseball league teams ceased to exist.

****

My grandfather, Julius O'Neil, was taken on a slave ship to America as a little boy.[1] He was given the name O'Neil which was the surname of the man who owned him at the time. After seeing what happened to other slaves, my grandfather admired the slave owner because the owner would oversee the slave personally and never broke up a family. My grandfather wasn't a bitter man, and felt that there was enough good in any white man to overcome racism.[2]

My grandmother was a petite gray-haired woman. She knew so many wonderful things to say to get you through things. When I was not allowed to go to a nearby high school because they only allowed white students, she would tell me, "John, they are in trouble because they are the ones who are treating you wrong while you are not treating them wrong. Don't be down because of that and hold your head high, because one day, even though I won't live to see it, you will be doing the same things that everyone else is doing."

There were only four high schools for black kids in the whole state of Florida. It bothered me that I could not attend the Sarasota High School, where we lived at the time, or matriculate at the University of Florida although my father paid taxes just like everyone else. That is what really hindered us because without education you do not have a chance.

My father started as a sawmill operator but lost his big toe in an accident while working. He then became a foreman of a crew on a celery farm. Most people only see celery in a store, and do not realize it grows in fields. After planting celery, and then having a plough cut it, you then have to strip it, which is backbreaking work in the heat of summer. One winter when I was home after the baseball season, a man tried to sell me his two-table poolroom. I decided to buy it and I got my daddy to run it because I was getting ready to play baseball again. When I came back the next year he had moved into a bigger building and had it going wonderful. He bought two more tables and had a store with cigars, cigarettes, candy, and stuff like that. He worked there until he died.

Playing baseball for the Kansas City Monarchs was an exciting time. We stayed in the best restaurants and hotels that just happened to be black-owned. I met the majority of the top entertainers of the time, as we played the same circuits they did. We would play Yankee Stadium and they would come to the ballgame and then at night we would see them entertain. At that time, all the theaters, hotels, and bars had live music — Duke Ellington might be playing one day and Count Basie the next.

A little-known fact is that there were more college-educated players in the Negro Leagues than in the Major Leagues. Forty percent of players were college-educated in our league because we always trained in a black college town and played the black colleges in spring training. The black colleges were like a minor league for us. We would take a player in the summer and they would go back to attending or teaching school in the winter.

There was a youngster who was playing with us, and he was a bright fellow and very inquisitive. Whenever I came down to breakfast, he would have the paper and would give it to me and say, "Tell me what happened in the majors," and I would. He would then get in the back of the bus and tell all the other players what happened in the major leagues with the paper in front of him. One day I saw him reading the paper bottom side up and I said to myself, "This kid can't read." I asked him about it and he said he wished he could. He was from the south, in cotton country, and during planting, chopping, and picking time, the school was closed so he had only three months out of the year to go to school. I got a primer and with Hilton Smith, who is in the Hall of Fame now, we taught him the alphabet. I would have him at night and Hilton would have him in the day, and when the baseball season was over he would go to school at night. He finally got his GED.

The lowest point for me was not on the baseball field but in the service. In World War II, I was in the Navy, in the Philippines, in a stevedore battalion where all the officers were white and all the people working were black. It was a form of slavery—really. A nice young man who was an officer out of Texas—you know he was white—said, "You know what, O'Neil? If you were white you would be an officer." He thought he was congratulating me on my work, but what it really meant to me was that I was qualified, and the only reason I was not an officer was because I was black! The only thing he could know about me is what his parents had taught him. When he got to know me, I was different than what he had pictured. I later became friends with him.

It was in the Philippines in 1945, that my commanding officer called me to his office at 11 p.m. and told me that Branch Rickey had just signed Jackie Robinson to an organized baseball contract. I said, "Thank God it finally happened — give me that microphone." I got on the microphone and said, "Hear this, hear this, hear this," which woke everyone up. I said, "Branch Rickey just signed Jackie Robinson to an organized baseball contract!" They hooped and hollered and shot guns, and we were so elated that it had finally happened, that no one slept much that night.

It was frustrating to see after the war that the rights of African-Americans had not changed. We returned home and found that despite fighting for freedom overseas, we were not given real freedom in our own country.

People always say to me, "Buck, I know you hated that you didn't get a chance to play major league baseball," and I say, "No, it did not bother me that I did not play major league baseball, because I played some of the best baseball in the country in the Negro leagues." Waste no tears for me. I didn't come along too early—I was right on time.[3]

My father always told me, "Anger will get you nothing. What you have to do is turn around the person who is doing you an injustice. You do this by being forgiving and loving. That will win them, more so than if you physically hit them because then they will hit you back. Then you get back nothing but a fight."

You have got to believe in yourself and don't ever stop trying. Never stop learning—I am 92 years old and I am still learning. Once you stop learning you are through—there is nothing else for you.

You have to have a faith and belief in God. Once you believe, it is so easy to love and forgive. When you give up anger, hatred, and prejudice, it frees you.[4] That is what it means to "give it up."

****

Integration started when Buck was 34 years of age and past his prime as a player, so he never got a chance to play in the white professional league. He joined the Major Leagues as a scout for the Chicago Cubs and later was named the Major's first black coach by the Cubs in 1962. Buck has since worked with the Kansas City Royals and is Chairman of the Negro Leagues Baseball Museum in Kansas City.

In 1995 he received one of his most prized possessions— an honorary diploma from Sarasota High School.

EPILOGUE

Almost every person I interviewed credited their faith with providing hope and strength in their darkest hours. This near universal response surprised me because I had randomly selected people to interview based on the type of adversity they had faced and I was unaware if they even believed that God existed. Opening my mind to the relationship between overcoming adversity and spiritual belief motivated me to learn more. I decided to read the Bible.

Each night I would read a few pages, curious as to why faith was so important to the individuals I had interviewed. At the same time, I was observing all the beauty evident in the nature reserve that surrounded my apartment in Minneapolis. I slowly came to the conclusion that the universe is more than just the product of a "big bang" and that God does exist.

Of course, one can overcome adversity without a spiritual focus or belief. I was able to extricate myself from a financial abyss completely on my own. However, as I look back at the years I was massively in debt, I can think of many times when a strong faith would have comforted me, and provided encouragement and hope. I was oblivious to this tremendous source of strength.

Regardless of the challenge you may be experiencing or the tragedy you are trying to overcome, you do not have to face it alone.

APPENDIX A

ADDITIONAL SOURCES OF INFORMATION

1) Gerald Coffee

Autobiography: Beyond Survival
Website: www.captaincoffee.com

2) Jackie Pflug

Autobiography: Miles To Go Before I Sleep
Website: www.jackiepflug.com

3) Drew Pearson

Website: www.drewpearsonmarketing.com

4) Brenda O'Quin

Website: www.pomcdfw.org
(Parents of Murdered Children)

5) Chuck Negron

Autobiography: Three Dog Nightmare
Website: www.negron.com
Website: www.cri-help.org

6) M'Liss and Chuck Switzer

Autobiography: Called To Account
http://home.att.net/~mlissbock/
DomesticViolence.html

7) Robert Grimminck

Autobiography: To Dream A Different Dream
Website: http://home.golden.net/
~rgrimminck/literacykit.html

8) Nora Lopez

Website: www.amnesty.ca (Amnesty International)

9) John Hiller

www.survivingadversity.com

10) Geraldine Ferraro

Autobiographies: Ferraro, My Story
Framing A Life

11) Mitch Berger

www.survivingadversity.com

12) Jason Weber

www.survivingadversity.com

13) Janet Guthrie	Autobiography: Autobiography pending Website: www.janetguthrie.com
14) Bill Rinaldi	Autobiography: You Can If You Think You Can Website: www.mdausa.org (Muscular Dystrophy Association)
15) Bob Love	Autobiography: The Bob Love Story
16) LuAn Mitchell-Halter	Website: www.luanmitchell.com
17) William Gregory	Website: www.innocenceproject.com
18) Jim McKenny	www.survivingadversity.com
19) Sarah Brady	Autobiography: A Good Fight Website: www.bradycampaign.org
20) Mike Utley	Website: www.mikeutley.org
21) Patty Wetterling	Website: www.jwf.org
22) Nick Brendon	Website: www.nickbrendon.com Website: www.stuttersfa.org
23) W Mitchell	Autobiography: It's Not What Happens To You, It's What You Do About It. Website: www.wmitchell.com
24) Terry-Jo Myers	Website: www.ichelp.com
25) Richard Sammons	Website: www.seeingeye.org
26) Diane MacWilliams	Website: www.quicksilvernow.com
27) Frank O'Dea	www.survivingadversity.com
28) Mary Stream	www.survivingadversity.com
29) John Steer	Autobiography: Wounded, A Reason To Live

30) Leslie Mouton   www.survivingadversity.com

31) Jim Smith   www.survivingadversity.com

32) Buck O'Neil   Autobiography: I Was Right On Time
                                       Website: www.nlbm.com
                                       (Negro Leagues Baseball Museum)

Other Helpful Websites:

Many of the organizations listed below also have regional, Canadian or local chapters and offices.

www.literacy.org

www.alcoholics-anonymous.org

www.na.org (narcotics anonymous)

www.gamblersanonymous.org

www.cancer.org

NOTES

CHAPTER FIVE

1. Chuck Negron with Chris Blatchford, Three Dog Nightmare (Los Angeles: Renaissance Books, 1999), 19
2. Negron with Blatchford, 22
3. Negron with Blatchford, 32, 33
4. Negron with Blatchford, 35
5. Negron with Blatchford, 36, 37
6. Negron with Blatchford, 41
7. Negron with Blatchford, 49
8. Negron with Blatchford, 42
9. Negron with Blatchford, 48
10. Negron with Blatchford, 53
11. Negron with Blatchford, 103
12. Negron with Blatchford, 120
13. Negron with Blatchford, 121
14. Negron with Blatchford, 143
15. Negron with Blatchford, 134
16. Negron with Blatchford, 155
17. Negron with Blatchford, 170
18. Negron with Blatchford, 201
19. Negron with Blatchford, 198
20. Negron with Blatchford, 223
21. Negron with Blatchford, 203
22. Negron with Blatchford, 213
23. Negron with Blatchford, 262
24. Negron with Blatchford, 283
25. Negron with Blatchford, 280
26. Negron with Blatchford, 329
27. Negron with Blatchford, 335